FOOD TRUCK BUSINESS

Complete Guide for Beginners. How to Start, Manage &
Grow Your Own Food Truck Business in 2020-2021

by

Ken Weber

TABLE OF CONTENTS

Introduction... 1

Chapter 1. The Basics Of Starting Up Your Own Food Truck....... 3

Chapter 2. Market Analysis 11

Chapter 3. Register With Government And Irs 22

Chapter 4. Benefits Of Owning A Food Truck Business............. 36

Chapter 5. Acquiring A Food Truck 40

Chapter 6: Food Safety 51

Chapter 7. Food Truck Vehicle Wraps 55

Chapter 8. Pros And Cons Of The Food Truck Lifestyle 61

Chapter 9. Customer Programs 66

Chapter 10. Foods You Can Get Started With....................... 75

Chapter 11. Plan Your Menu 139

Chapter 12. Marketing Your Truck 148

Chapter 13. Tips To Keep The Food Truck Running 163

Chapter 14. Profits And Expenses 168

Chapter 15. Qualities That A Food Truck Vendor Must Have... 173

Chapter 16. Pitfalls To Avoid 175

Conclusion 178

INTRODUCTION

A re you the kind of individual who knows there's a lot more out there than only an hourly job? Do you realize you could make it all alone in the event that you simply had a plan to follow? If this is the case, the food truck business could be the perfect decision for you.

If you've ever dreamed of starting your own food truck business, be ready for an experience that will challenge you to the extremes, and also create satisfaction like nothing else! If you ask random business owners, you'll find that there are endless stories of early struggles just to make it to launch day. But how do everyday people accomplish such a goal? Business owners come from all types of industries and backgrounds. Most of them start their own businesses to achieve the freedom to work for themselves. This freedom often means independence, more significant earning potential, and a sense of fulfillment that can only come from building a successful business.

Believe me; food trucks are here to stay because they are out-satisfying customers who frequent brick and mortar restaurants. As we will discuss further, exceptional food trucks meet consumer needs better than existing restaurants.

The bubbly persona of food truck operators engaging with customers is an experience not usually encountered by patrons ordering food from a drive-thru window or while seated at a restaurant. The person customers interact with at the window of a

1

food truck is often the owner, and this individual is passionate about what they do, and it shows through the way they interact with the customer.

One of the industries that can offer all that and more is the mobile food industry! The popularity of gourmet food trucks has exploded for both consumers and owners. In fact, food truck programs on television are further fueling the interest in this fast-growing and profitable industry. If you've watched these programs or experienced the excitement around mobile kitchens in person, then you can see why so many people are turning to the streets to create their next business.

To start a business, you need adequate funding. And just as the mobile food industry sets the trends in high tech food marketing, other high-tech industries are helping many food truck owners to generate the capital they need to get their ideas off the ground.

Through crowdfunding, a business owner could fully fund or partially fund a project to obtain the capital needed without the hassles of a traditional loan. This is not necessarily a simple task! There are specific guidelines to follow to increase your chances of success. The goal of this book is to show you specific tips you can integrate into your food truck crowdfunding project so you can join the entrepreneurs before you who have obtained startup capital through this innovative funding platform. Let's get started!

CHAPTER 1. THE BASICS OF STARTING UP YOUR OWN FOOD TRUCK

Food truck concessions are intended to enable you to own your own business and serve top-notch food without having to deal with the high cost and hassle of owning an eatery. In any case, not all food truck businesses are of similar quality.

At top mobile food franchises, you will get the experience of a demonstrated innovator in the quick casual food market. You begin with every one of the instruments you have to succeed, including a solid business framework that you have access, from the minute you consent to your Franchise Arrangement. What's more, these top franchises won't leave you out there all alone. You'll experience a broad training program system to enable you to succeed.

Are you concerned about permit or hiring? Try not to be. The best mobile concessions will have frameworks set up for the work planning process just as full direction through permits and zoning. You'll appreciate electronic detailing and your very own food cost analysis framework so you can invest your energy serving your clients, not managing heaps of paperwork.

Starting a food truck business is an energizing endeavor that doesn't require a huge money expense. You can search for low start-up expenses to guarantee you'll be experiencing your fantasy in as little as 90 days. You'll be offering your clients mobile food concessions, unlike others. You can serve sought after foods like Vermont Farms Natural Chicken, grass-fed Vermont meat burgers, healthy vegetable wraps, and top-quality frozen yogurt. The present day's top mobile food franchises are on the road to success to quick easygoing food success. The mobile food trailer business is getting a charge out of astounding development (14%, and that's only the tip of the iceberg!) incredible in these challenging economic times. You can be a part of that achievement.

The meals truck enterprise is one of the fastest-growing industries for a purpose. The company is pretty smooth for marketers to recognize, at the equal time as clients cannot seem to get enough of food vans of their towns. So, now which you see how popular food cars may be, how can any properly-which means person get started out with their very personal meals truck business?

To begin, even though starting a food truck is considered simpler than beginning a restaurant, it's nevertheless hard to get off the floor if you're now not prepared to place within the effort to make it work. Meals trucks can end up exceedingly at risk of succumbing to the factors and be difficult to many different risky outdoor factors like special cars, theft, vandalism, and even sudden fireplace dangers.

Every so often, running a food truck during certain seasons is grounds for now not getting any income. I advise you do not want to run your food truck in the winter... whilst you are promoting mostly frozen treats like ice cream. The hours can be lengthy, too—some food vehicles stay out from 9 inside the morning to as last as 5 in the afternoon on an ordinary time table, even as others turn out to be spending the entire day and night time in a single spot.

Regardless of those real troubles, beginning a food truck stays a superb manner to get began out as an entrepreneur is well known. And, if you're particularly obsessed with meals, possibly starting a meals truck can be very a great deal for you.

Questions to Ask Yourself Before Opening a Food Truck

Starting any business takes time. Even though, so long as you make an effort to start a business, you ought not to fear any capacity faults that can arise when running the business itself. That notion additionally applies to folks who count on to get into the mobile food industry, although they don't anticipate to get concerned in the enterprise... until they're approximately to make contributions.

Though, before you determine out what form of meals truck you are planning to open, it's essential to invite yourself questions about what you could assume out of this business.

Those questions may include:

- What's my passion for food?

- What type of food do I want to serve?

- What type of food may be missing from my community?

- Are there other food trucks with the same concepts/food products like mine?

- How can I differentiate my brand from other brands?

- How much money will I have to invest in this business initially?

- Where am I going to get the food that I'm planning to serve in my business?

- How much do I need to invest in those products?

Asking questions allows put off the uncertainty related to beginning a food truck enterprise. For numerous people, understanding greater approximately what to expect from a meals truck business makes them greater relaxed with beginning the enterprise inside the first location, in view that they do know what to anticipate after doing the studies.

Once you analyze extra approximately what to anticipate, there are different elements that you have to take into consideration, especially while you're, you guessed it, considering beginning a meals truck enterprise. Quite a few of these factors are a quite crucial part of the enterprise itself, making it quite vital to take note of them.

The Most Integral Factors of Starting a Food Truck Business

The essential factors of beginning a meals truck company are quite straightforward when you recall it. They're very lots the identical factors concerned with starting different businesses because you quite load want to attend to the one's matters earlier than taking off on the road for the primary time!

The intensity with which these elements are confronted is something that we will cover in the following sections if you wish to apprehend it. Though, earlier than then, let's take a look at the ones elements, as paraphrased from a mobile food agency useful resource:

Legalities

Understandingly, you can't precisely run a meals truck business without looking a few permit forms from your city and country jurisdiction. Having permissions without a doubt is specially designed to cowl a mobile agency looks after, nicely, the legalities associated with strolling such an enterprise and operating the automobile interior your city.

At remarkable, a permit safely covers strolling most elements of your mobile food truck, besides you want greater criminal permissions from your city or county jurisdiction.

Since the advent of the gourmet food truck, menus and food choices are far beyond the earlier days of standard burgers, sandwiches, and tacos. With a growing number of new food trucks serving various specialty foods and an array of cultures providing influence, county and city licenses have also needed updating. Some cities are faster to adopt this new type of business, while for other cities, old regulations and resistance from brick-and-mortar restaurants and other groups have slowed down the growth in this booming industry.

Each city and location is different, so it's best to conduct additional research to find what permits and licenses are necessary for your area. However, there are general procedures to follow in terms of finding and obtaining the proper licenses and registrations.

Vehicles

Manifestly, you want to discover a truck to conduct and deliver your business everywhere you want it to adventure. Now, you ought to spend plenty of cash on a food truck. Many food-prepared trucks and trailers can fee as low as USD 1,500 and as high as $75,000, depending on the type of truck you can plan to buy ultimately.

In the end, you need to head for a truck or food-organized vehicle it's miles big enough to house the company and remaining some time.

Logo

If you need your food truck to be eye-catching, you will need to establish a brand. A brand is what allows customers the ability to properly understand the business, especially if that business is already well known. As a food truck proprietor, you are going to want human beings to recollect the decision of your business and the ingredients you eat, so begin brainstorming names and thoughts that might foster what you envision your enterprise being.

Names also are just one a part of setting up a business; you also have to give you a viable menu, decide out what additives and meals to buy, and put together whatever you need to address earlier than even getting the legal paperwork out of the way.

Financing

Arguably the maximum important issue of starting a meals truck. Why? It's far, in particular because you absolutely cannot do loads with little to no financing. You cannot even purchase the truck! So, in advance, then you get into the entire planning issue, search for capacity non-public groups.

You could have the exceptional desirable fortune looking for a private investor who can be interested in backing your food truck business, even though that rarely occurs till an investor definitely takes location to love your imaginative and prescient and your food.

You could typically head to your financial institution to get a loan, specifically if you qualify for any of their financing options. Naturally, you could typically be searching for help from an opportunity monetary corporation if you do now not want to apply to a bank.

Financing a food truck normally consists of protective expenses for the truck, branding, system, food and its associated additives, point-of-sale (POS) or credit score card systems, protection precautions, and, every so often, employees.

So, as you could see, several factors bypass into starting your private food truck business. At the same time, as we surely protected the ones particular factors in brief right here, we will evaluation those standards and boom on them a hint greater presently. Even though, for now, it allows taking a look at your alternatives close to beginning your very own meals truck business.

Business Plan

A formal written business plan is generally necessary when seeking funding from banks or investors. If you are financing your own business, it is not required; however, it is important to think about and make notes on each part. You may find it helpful to write it out and have your thoughts together in one place. Following is a simple guide to the business plan and its parts.

For a business to succeed, there should be a pretty backed-up business plan. You should know how to put an effective business plan when it comes to this type of business. There should be a decent clarity in what you want to do and how you want to do it.

Executive Summary

The Executive Summary should be written last. It takes all of the information from the other portions of the plan and creates a short explanation of the business and your vision for it. This should be a short description that is a few paragraphs long. This is where you make your "elevator speech" to the bank and investors. Be positive and convincing.

This is going to be a brief proposal of your business plan to target the audience. You should know what you are going to serve, where you are going to serve it, and why it will be amazing in the area that you have chosen. You should also look past the present and see the big picture of your future in this business. You should be sure about the plan. You should plan accordingly if you want to reproduce the same idea with several food trucks all over the country in the upcoming years.

Company Description

This title speaks for itself. This section dives into more details of the business, such as structure, ownership, location, etc. This is the area to describe why you started the business. Tell your story here, and include the details of who, when, where, why, and how. Also, include your mission and vision statements as well as financial and growth goals.

Products and Services

This is where you will detail your menu. You can talk about the experience you want to give your customers. For example, if you plan to work wedding receptions, you can describe your "wedding package" that serves high electrolyte drinks and starchy foods to combat hangovers. Include how you can personalize. Make sure you describe your products in an intriguing way that shows why they should be purchased and why your target market will be excited to buy them.

Don't forget to include complementary products. This could include shirts, hats, coffee, etc.

CHAPTER 2. MARKET ANALYSIS

Market Analysis is very important. You do not want to open a Food Truck in a town or area that is already saturated. You will want to understand your competition and differentiate yourself from them. The most successful businesses are experts in their specific niche. If you are a food truck that sells tacos, and there are already three other food trucks that sell tacos in your area, you may want to consider changing your offerings to something different, such as barbeque or a burrito that tastes great.

Look at trends and see what people are buying. For example, bacon went through a stage where it was all the rage. Be sure to take advantage of trends, but also be sure your product is sustainable. Also, watch trends in other parts of the country. Stay up to date on industry news. You will want to offer a new trend first if you can!

You will want to describe your target market in this section as well. For example, if your main focus is weddings, you will focus on reaching brides, who may be between 20-35 years old, and their mothers, who may be between 40-65 years old. You can include information such as income, age, race, religion, or any other demographic that applies.

It is also an important part of the plan, and it will be solely based on the extent to which you research the specific market. This type of analysis is essential in understanding the strategies that can be followed to get a hold of the market that you are getting into. When getting into the mobile food truck industry, these are the key points that should be duly covered:

- Current trends, growth rate, and consumer data in the food industry.

- Age group, geography of the area, socioeconomic factors, and other demographic information of the audience in the target.

- Need of the market and any specific seasonal or regional trends that might affect the market.

- Structure of pricing, total margin levels, and other financial information.

- List of potential customers and how to gain their confidence in the present situation and in the future.

- Hurdles and problems in setting up the joint.

- Knowledge about regulations such as food codes that have to be complied with and how would you work to meet the requirements.

- Also include expected market changes, such as weddings in Spring, Summer, and Fall, and slow times in winter, depending on your location.

In order to conduct a market analysis, you will need to do these five steps:

Decide the Purpose of Your Market Study

This seems obvious, but you want to determine how likely it is that you will have success and prevent any future problems.

Determine Target Customers

Your target customers will be your repeat customers. Determine your target customers, then research the needs, interests, and demographics of this group.

Gather Data for Conducting a Market Analysis

The more information you gather the better prepared you will be. Be sure your data is factual and unbiased. You may feel the urge to ignore negative data, but the more you know in the beginning results in better decision making later.

Some places you can get data from:

- Bureau of Labor Statistics

- State and local commerce websites

- Articles in trade journals

- Interviews, focus groups, questionnaires, and surveys from your target market and trade associations.

Competitor Strengths and Weaknesses

Analyze your information. With the data you have gathered, you can project how well a product will sell, a cash flow cycle, and more. You should describe the industry as a whole, including size, growth rate, and major customer groups. Describe target market traits, including buying habits, demographics, and projected growth. You will want to include your competitor analysis, including competitor strengths and weaknesses, and market share. You will also want to mention any regulatory issues you may encounter and how you will deal with them.

Put your market analysis to work. Use your market analysis for planning and to make adjustments in your business. Be prepared to talk about your market analysis to investors and banks if you need them. This is a tool that will help you be successful. It should be revised at least annually.

Strategy and Implementation

Strategy and Implementation are all about how you are will do things and how you plan to make it work. You will want to research competitor's pricing, cost of supplies and determine prices using that information. You will want to base prices on the following equation: Cost + Profit = Price. The Cost portion needs to include all costs (rent, utilities, loans, payroll, and supplies). If you have to borrow a lot to get started, that will either raise your prices or eat into your profits. Be sure always to pay yourself a fair rate as well. Business owners in general work long hours and are not always paid well at first. This is where planning becomes so important. Plan to build your salary and profit into the cost of your products.

Once you determine your costs, you determine how much profit you want to make. You can choose any percentage you want, and it may be influenced by the competitor's pricing, the amount of debt you have, etc. It is recommended that you build at least some profit in and save that amount for when you have a slow time, an unexpected tax bill, etc. You will need it at some point.

An example of pricing:

Costs per month:

- Rent $750

- Utilities $250

- Owner's salary $4200

- Insurance $150

- Supplies $2000

- Advertising $500

- Total costs $7850

- Add 10% for profit $7850 + $785

If you are open six days a week, you divide this number by 26, which equals $332.12. This is the magic number that you need to meet each day you are open. You may find that this is your daily average after a week if you have a really slow Monday and Tuesday but then are swamped on Saturday.

To price your individual products, you need to estimate how many of each product you plan to sell. Let's say you sell donuts, and you sell them by the dozen, and each dozen is $15. To meet your expenses, you will need to sell 23 dozen to meet your daily goal of $332.12. If you think you are more likely to sell 20 dozen, you adjust your price to $16.60 (20 items at $16.60 =$332).

Now, if you find out that the Food Truck down the street is charging $18 a dozen for a similar product, you could adjust up and maybe add more profit. If the Food Truck down the street is charging $13 a dozen, you will need to find a way to cut costs or be sure you are selling a superior product.

If you have several different products, you just have to estimate how many of each product you think you will sell each day and build that into your equation. For example, if you have cakes and donuts for sale, you may plan to sell three cakes a day and 15 dozen donuts. You can get very technical with how much time and supply cost goes into each item, or you can estimate using the total you need to sell each day. In this example, if each cake is $20 (total $60), then each dozen donuts must be $18. Or, if each cake is $22, then each dozen needs to be $17.73. Again, if these prices are too high, you need to find a place to cut costs. You will want to cut your salary or profit first but resist that feeling! There is almost always somewhere else to cut costs; keeping the emergency fund is very important!

Once you determine your products and pricing, you need to decide how you are going to sell them. You have many options, including a brick and mortar location, delivery, food truck, or internet sales (depending on your state regulations).

Your target market is going to determine your marketing and sales strategy. If you are targeting brides, you will want to go to bridal shows, give samples, perhaps partner with other wedding vendors for referrals, and do social media marketing. Each target market will have its own ideal marketing strategy. Grandparents do not find products the same way young parents do. Just because your family and friends promise to shop at your Food Truck constantly, they will likely not be buying the 15-20 dozen donuts every day that you need to meet your sales minimum. You will need to find new customers.

There are many ways to market your business. This book goes into more detail later, but some options for marketing are events, social media, newspapers, mailings, tv commercials, and more. You need to establish a strategy and a budget and BE CONSISTENT.

This section of the business plan is where you describe your pricing and sales strategy. It is good to include enough detail to show that your business will be sustainable and profitable.

Organization and Management Team

In this section, you describe your Organization and Management Team. This could be a team of one or a team of several. You should also describe your plans for your team as your business grows. Maybe you have a goal of starting very small and growing as demand grows. Perhaps you are already at the point that you need additional help. Whatever your vision is, describe it in detail here.

Management is key when starting any business. Detail any management experience you or your management team has. Highlight the expertise and qualifications of each member if you don't have any experience, research management methods. There are many books out there to help you. Some recommended titles are listed in the Resources section at the end of the book.

Financial Plan and Projections

This section is designed to help you understand how much money you will need and how much you will make. If you are seeking funding from a bank or investor, this is the section that shows how much you need.

The first step to this section is to determine how much you need to get started. For a Food Truck, you will need to meet state and local regulations for food production. You will have to have an inspection, then be granted a permit. You can find your state and local information pretty easily by googling "food production and sales permit in my state." Once you determine how much you will need to spend getting this, you can start looking at costs for other requirements, such as sales tax permits, state filing requirements, and more. All of this can be overwhelming, but it does help to write it all down with the costs so that you know what you need to get started.

Once you have all of the legal and regulatory issues taken care of, it is time to look at overhead costs. These costs include accounting fees, advertising, insurance, legal fees, interest, rent, supplies, utilities, and travel costs.

Then you determine what your direct costs will be. These are labor, material, and expenses related to producing your goods and services.

Once you have compiled all of your expenses, you can break it down yearly, monthly, and daily. This helps to know if you are on track or not.

Next, you will estimate your income. If you have already been in business for a while, you will have data that you can use to do this. If not, you can estimate based on what you found during your market analysis.

With this information, you can project how much you will be able to make and what your funding needs will be. Be sure that your calculations are showing enough profit to pay back the money that you are borrowing. If the numbers aren't working, you will need to go back and change your plans to ensure success.

See the below example (yearly):

- Startup Costs

- Food permit, legal filings, etc. $500

- Deposits: $1500

- Overhead costs:

- Accounting fees: $1200

- Advertising: $6000

- Insurance: $1800

- Legal fees $500

- Rent: $9000

- Utilities: $3000

- Travel (truck costs): $3600

- Total Overhead: $25,600

- Direct Costs:

- Labor: $50,400

- Expenses: $24,000

- Total Direct Costs: $74,400/year

- Total Costs (Startup + Overhead + Direct Costs): $102,000/year

- $8500/month

- $326.92/day

I like to add profit to that. For this example, we will use 10%. Some banks and investors may not want this included.

- Total with profit:

- $112,200/year

- $9350/month

- $360/day

Now that you know what your costs are, you can estimate what your income will be. If you have already been making sales, you will have an idea of what to expect. Perhaps you have orders already on the books and can expect more of the same. If you are going in totally blind, refer to your market analysis to estimate your sales.

To determine this, we will go backward from how we determined the daily costs and start with the daily income. Using the example before, we have a dozen donuts for $15 and cakes for $22. We are expecting one wedding order per week for $300. We will divide this by days, putting $50 on each day. Then we plan to sell 20 dozen donuts and three cakes. This brings our total to $300 in donuts, $66 in cakes, and $50 for the wedding booking, equaling $412 for the day.

Total daily income: $412

$10,712/month

$128,544/year

This analysis shows that you will have plenty of money left over to make payments or pay investors. Many times, you will need to show growth and create five years of projections. If you plan to grow 20% per year, simply add 20% to the total for each year, then divide by 12 for the monthly amount, and then by 26 days for a Food Truck that is open six days per week.

Legal Business Structure

When it comes to choosing a legal business structure, it is a good idea to understand all your options. What you choose can have a big impact on your business with taxes and legal issues. There are pros and cons to each choice. Below we will discuss your options.

Sole Proprietorship

A Sole Proprietorship is a business owned by a single person. In this setup, there is no legal distinction between the person and the business. This is the simplest choice; however, it leaves you open to lawsuits if something goes wrong with the business. You are also personally responsible for any debts incurred by the business. Also, income and losses for the business are taxed on the owner's individual income tax returns. If you have a DBA (Doing Business As) name, you may need to register it with local or state authorities. For example, your name is Casey Entrepreneur, but your Food Truck is called ABC Food Truck. You need to register ABC Food Truck as your DBA.

Partnership

A Partnership is created when two or more partners start a business. This is very similar to the Sole Proprietorship in that the owners report profits and losses on their individual income tax return. A Partnership must file an informational return as well. The partnership is also similar to the Sole Proprietorship in the way that it leaves you open to lawsuits and liabilities. You will need to file a Certificate of Limited Partnership with the state. This certificate describes the basics of your limited partnership. Not every state requires it, and sometimes it is called something else. Check with your Secretary of State for details. You should also create a Limited Partnership Agreement, which is an internal binding document that spells out each partner's duties and responsibilities. This document is not always required but is HIGHLY recommended. You may have a great relationship with your partner at the beginning, but things can change quickly. You will want to have clearly identified responsibilities from the beginning.

Limited Liability Company

A Limited Liability Company is formed to protect the Sole Proprietor and Partnerships from lawsuits. These protect the owner(s) when something goes wrong. For example, two partners open an auto repair shop and make a mistake while changing a tire. The wheel falls off going down the road, and the driver is injured; they can only sue the shop for damages up to the assets of the LLC. They will not be able to sue the individual owners for their personal assets.

Limited liability companies require the Articles of Organization. This is a simple document that describes the basic outline of your business. You should also prepare an LLC Operating Agreement. It is not required in every state but is highly recommended. It lays out how key business decisions are made and each member's duties and responsibilities. This document will protect you if any disagreements arise between members.

CHAPTER 3. REGISTER WITH GOVERNMENT AND IRS

This part of starting a business can seem overwhelming and intimidating. This guide will take you through the steps that you need to take at each level of government to get you open for business.

Local

Whether or not you need to register with your local government depends completely on location. Most do not require a specific registration, but more likely a permit or license. Check your local government websites to ensure you are in compliance with requirements.

Federal

Generally, the only reasons small businesses need to engage the federal government is to apply for a federal tax ID number, get trademark protection, or tax-exempt status. You can apply for your federal tax ID number online, and takes only minutes in most cases.

Sales Tax

If your business sells products or services that are subject to sales tax, you will need to apply for a sales tax permit. If you are not sure if your product or service requires sales tax, you can find out on the Small Business Administration website, sba.gov. If you sell items online, you may be subject to tax as well. Be sure to understand your state's requirements.

Sales tax payments are due either monthly or quarterly, depending on your sales volume. This will be determined when you apply for your permit. It is a good idea to keep your sales tax in a separate bank account than your general operating account, especially if you are operating on a tight budget. It can be too easy to borrow from this money, and the government isn't keen on loaning its money out. You will be penalized for late payments.

Employee Sales Withholding

If you are going to have employees, you have to withhold federal and state taxes (in most states) from their paychecks. The employee must fill out a W-4 before they start work. This will determine how much needs to be withheld. Employees may ask how to fill out the W-4. It is good practice to recommend the employee consults an accountant if they are not sure.

If you are using accounting software, you can enter the employee's information, and it will tell you what to withhold for the employee's state, federal, Social Security, etc. Some software will file the required forms for you, and the payments will be automatically pulled from your bank account. Some recommended software is listed in the Resources section at the end of the book.

Talk to an accountant to ensure you are withholding the correct amount from everyone's pay, as well as you are paying the matching portions. You will also be required to pay FUTA, which is federal unemployment insurance.

Permits

Depending on your location, there could be a variety of permits that you might need for your business. It is important to research these with your city and county government websites. You may need a variance or conditional use permit if your location is not zoned for business. This is especially important to check into if you are running your business from home.

You may need a Fire Department permit depending on the type of business and location you have. Many cities have Air and Water Pollution permits that businesses must have now. You also may be subject to a Sign Permit, depending on your city.

If you are located outside of a city, you may be subject to similar county regulations.

Licensing

Licensing is similar to permits in that it is usually determined by your location. Business licenses are generally granted by the city, usually with a fee.

Professional licensing is usually handled by the state. Food services are highly regulated and usually subject to inspections. Be sure to check with your state licensure website before starting any operations.

It's a very basic guideline that before you get on the road and set up your Food Truck business, you have to get a license first. It's one of the non-negotiables when it comes to this kind of business, especially because you really do not want to deal with the authorities asking you why you're parking your truck in an open space with a lot of people around. Remember, a food truck is a business that is situated in a truck, and of course, a truck is a vehicle that takes up a lot of space, so it's just right that you get a license to make everything legal.

If you're planning to start a business in the coming year, make sure that you file for your license before January as there usually is a long waitlist of people who want to obtain licenses in the said month and you certainly wouldn't want to be part of that. Furthermore, you should also check with your local government unit about requirements as they differ from each state. When you do this, everything will be easy.

However, there are a couple of things that are most similar when it comes to licenses for food business, and these are:

- Food Manager Identification Card from your district.

- Proper Identification and Proof of Ownership.

- Food Record Keeping.

- Food Storage Record.

- Business Plan.

- Copy of a written message of support from your community leaders.

Once you obtain all these and contact your local government units for further information, you're all set to have your license!

So, now that you have a license, you should now get your own truck—and decide what you want to sell!

Purchase an Insurance Policy

An insurance policy will likely be one of the most important things you purchase for your business. Protecting yourself against liability is extremely important and can prevent potential personal and professional financial ruin.

General Liability

You will definitely want to purchase a general liability policy. This will protect you against injuries sustained because of your business. This means if someone gets hurt in your truck or because of your products, you are covered. Slips and falls, food poisoning, etc. should be covered under this policy. Be sure to have your insurance agent go through the policy with you to be sure it includes everything you need.

Umbrella Insurance

Umbrella insurance is something you should consider if you are working as a sole proprietor. Sole proprietors are left open to personal lawsuits since they are legally responsible for the business and its debts. An umbrella policy goes above and beyond the limits of your current policies. It can be a good idea for anyone, but especially those with this type of business structure. Again, your insurance agent can give you your options when it comes to any insurance policy.

Professional Liability

Professional Liability is needed when you can make errors that do not necessarily cause physical or personal harm. This type of insurance covers businesses in the case of negligence, misrepresentation, violation of good faith, etc. Errors and Omissions policies are a type of professional liability insurance.

Worker's Compensation

Worker's Compensation insurance is required if you have employees. This insurance protects you against damages in the instance that an employee is injured on the job. Be sure to teach your employees about safety and enforce your policies! Not only do you want to prevent an injury to an employee, but a claim can be very expensive for a long time, so make sure to make safety a priority.

Unemployment Insurance

Unemployment insurance is also mandatory if you have employees. It is usually run through your state. It exists so that when people are laid off or fired from their jobs, they can still collect a paycheck. Your rates will go up with a lot of usage, so try to avoid these claims if you can. If you have a problem employee, be sure to follow your policy on discipline and keep good notes on what is happening. This way, you can show that you did your best with the employee, and they were not willing to follow the rules, show up, etc. Terminating employees is never fun, but you have to protect yourself in the process. Links to policy templates are included in the Resources section at the end of the book.

Location

Choosing a great location is extremely important to your success. Depending on your business model and local regulations, you could have several options to start your business. You could start at home, in a small, off the beaten path location, or something larger in a busy area. There is no wrong or right answer; you just have to prepare for whichever option you choose properly. We will discuss the pros and cons of all of them.

Next, you have to choose where you'd like to set up your truck. There are certain areas that attract food truck loyalists more than others, and these are those places that you have to target. These are:

Famous Tourist Destinations

Why? Well, exactly because you know that people will be flocking around the area! There's definitely a place in your town that people usually frequent and that people from all over the world visit. If you can get a permit to set your truck up there, then you'd be on the right track. And, if this is the case, you might as well sell foods that are connected to your area or food that your area is known for so you can be sure that people will try what you have to offer.

Malls or Shopping Districts

Again, there are a lot of people around these areas, and everyone knows that shopping isn't for the faint of heart. Sometimes, people go from shop to shop, and that's very tiring, so of course, they'd get tired and hungry, and when the lines are too long in the restaurants at the mall, they will look for somewhere else to eat—such as your food truck! This way, they can also bond with their family or friends more and have fun choosing orders from your menu!

Empty Lots

It's simple: when a lot is empty, there's a lot that you can do with it. Before a restaurant gets built or before people loiter around the area with nothing to do, why don't you get a license and set your truck up there? It's a good way to make money and attract people to try something new instead of just sitting around and doing nothing. Think of the empty lot as an empty mind—it's so open for possibilities, and that's what you want your business to have! This way, it'll be easy for people to associate the lot with your food truck, and they'll find it as a great place to hang around in.

Office Parking Lots

Working at an office is not always easy. There are times when the workload is just too much that one is forced to take back their food to their cubicle with them. In this case, they need to be able to eat somewhere nice and different, just to get away from the monotony of it all, but they also have to make sure that they won't burn a hole in their pockets. As for this, you may want to put up your food truck in an office parking lot so that office workers won't have to go far just to eat lunch or get themselves some snacks. As there are loads of office workers and long office hours, you can be sure that you'll definitely earn a lot! In fact, during lunchtime alone, you'll probably be able to get most of your capital back, so this is definitely a good place for you to put your truck in.

Business Districts

Don't stick to one office alone—target the whole business district. This way, when people are out of their offices for an hour or so, they can just check out your food truck and eat something or buy something that they can take with them on the go!

College Campuses

You know how college kids want to try everything, right? So, of course, when they see a food truck around the campus or even just a couple of blocks away, they'll definitely be rushing to try what you have to offer—which is a good thing for your business. Plus, in this age of social media, they'll surely post photos of your truck and your products online, which is a great form of free advertising for you!

Train and Bus Stations

These are places where people have to wait for their ride, and more often than not, they'll be looking for something that they could munch on. So, when they see your food truck, they'll feel as if their prayers have been answered, and they'll be thankful that you're there to save them from their misery!

Beaches

Not all people have the time to prepare food for beach trips. Sometimes, they just want to go there, and of course, it would also be hard if they spend all their money on restaurants around the area as they may be too pricey. But, with your food truck around, they have an alternative to the usual fruits or kebobs, and surely, they'll be able to enjoy that.

Events or Festivals

Make yourself available and send your plans to event organizers. Chances are, they'll allow you to set up your truck in a certain festival or event because there are a lot of people around and of course, they wouldn't just spend their time listening to the bands, they'd also want something to eat—so you have to be able to give them what they want.

Sports Events

Imagine it's an outdoor setting, great. But, if it's an indoor setting, that's okay, too. Just wait for the event to finish or be there before it starts, so while people are waiting in line, they can order some food from you, and they won't just stand there being bored.

Remember, before you park your truck in any of these spaces, make sure that you have the license and that you have talked to the right people so everything will be official, and you won't have any problems.

At-Home

With a Food Truck, you need to make sure this is an option in your location. Generally, you must have a separate kitchen for your business, or at the very least, keep all of your personal pans and supplies separate from your business. There is no sharing the flour from your cookies for sale with your flour for pancakes on Saturday morning with the family.

However, there are obvious benefits to having your business start at home. You could easily work another job and start slowly marketing your services. You will have very low overhead costs since you are already paying for your household expenses. You can start spending an hour or two a day in the evenings with marketing and booking work. Once you have a good client base and enough work to sustain your full-time employment, you can leave your day job and devote all of your time to your business.

You will eventually outgrow your home space and will need to rent a more professional space, but you should have enough money saved to make the transition fairly easily if you follow the plan laid out in this book. The length of time it takes to get there is dependent on how serious you are about your business. Later in the book, we will discuss ways to become financially independent and how to level up in your business. A professional space is the next level in an at-home business.

The drawbacks to the In-Home business model is that you will not have traffic from the street or from signs. You will need to be marketing to keep your audience's attention constantly.

Small and Cheap

Small and Cheap is another option. Small and Cheap is usually off the beaten path, and the rent is low. This is recommended for business owners that are jumping in full time and want a physical location. It can also be a stepping stone between In-Home and Large and In-Charge.

There are benefits and drawbacks to this option, just like the others. Some of the benefits include having a professional space and signage for that 24 hour a day marketing presence. This is the kind of presence you need for people to say, "Oh, we could call that Food Truck business down on Third Street!" when they are searching for a service like yours.

With Small and Cheap, part of the strategy is not to break the bank on the rent. Your location may not be ideal. You may have to drive a few extra miles to get there, and it might not be the prettiest building. However, saving money is key in this stage. You will want to be sure you will be able to show a profit before signing a lease. It is vital to do a financial analysis before entering this stage. Once expenses become significant (i.e., rent and utilities), you are putting yourself at the risk of losing money. You could also MAKE a lot of money! You just have to plan to succeed.

Large and In-Charge

If you are ready to go all-in and rent the large space with potential foot traffic, you want to go Large and In-Charge! This option will take quite a bit more money than the others, so you may need to secure a loan or line of credit before jumping in. This plan will also likely need a larger staff, so you may not be able to go it alone. It is recommended to have a detailed business plan before making this move.

The pros of this are extensive. You will have foot traffic and signage to advertise your business 24 hours a day, seven days a week. You can hold marketing events in your space. You will look like a professional and serious business. There will be a buzz around your grand opening, and people will want to stop in to see for themselves the new place in town.

The cons mostly revolve around one thing: money. Your new space will be expensive. You will have a large monthly rent payment, as well as higher utilities. You will have to pay the staff. If the buzz wears off quickly, and you have failed to create a consistent customer base, you will run out of money quickly. You absolutely must meet daily goals or start scaling back quickly!

This option isn't for everyone. You just must be prepared for anything that can happen and have a contingency plan ready! You could be very successful or fail very quickly.

Ways to Save Money

No matter what option you choose, a smart businessperson will try to keep expenses low. You must always be thinking of slow periods. Even if you are swamped during certain times of the year, you will likely experience a slowdown at another point during the year. There are several ways to save money, depending on what location you choose.

Some ideas are below:

- Use your personal cell phone instead of a landline.

- Keep thermostat set high or low, depending on the season. If you are not there, be sure you are using energy-saving measures.

- Buy used equipment.

- Get free software.

- Barter with vendors.

- Buy supplies in bulk.

- Hire only part-time help to save on benefit costs.

Entrepreneur Spirit

When you think of an entrepreneur, you think of someone on the move, motivated by the dream of independence, money, and most importantly, being their own boss! So many entrepreneurs fail because they have plenty of dreams, just not enough practical business sense to make things work. You have to keep the dream; just be sure to spend the time learning the hard stuff. That is the stuff that will bring you and your business to its knees if you are not prepared. It is not something that most people know, so pay attention!

According to the SBA.gov, 30% of businesses fail within the first two years, 50% during the first five years, and 66% within the first ten years. One of the hardest things to do while in the thick of starting a business is to see past the next payroll. You have to be able to plan for hard times and not go crazy when you get your first big check. Yes, you should celebrate victories big and small, but if you want to be in it for the long haul, you must be smart about spending.

There are five parts to the Entrepreneur Spirit. They are:

They Are In-Tune with Their Passion

No matter how well or poorly you seem to be doing, remember why you are doing it. Do you love frosting cookies? Do you love to see people's faces when they see your delicious creations? What is your end goal? Reflecting on why you are doing it always keeps you in touch with your passion. Your mindset determines your success. Imagine yourself in 3 or 5 years living your dream. There are plenty of Entrepreneur Mindset books out there. I recommend reading a couple if you are not already practicing a positive mindset. There are several listed in the Resources section of the book that are amazing. Your mindset can be a game-changer!

They Are Always Questioning How It Can Be Done Better

Entrepreneur minds never rest. If you feel a process isn't working as well as it could, you will be thinking about how to make it more efficient, more personalized, etc. This process is vital to keeping you fresh and on your toes. If you feel something isn't working well, talk to a trusted advisor or friend that is also in business or management. Seeing other's points of view can help spark the answer in you. You do not have to take other's advice, but talking it out can bring clarity to your mind in many cases.

Optimistic About All Possibilities

Optimism is key in business. If someone asks you to do something outside your comfort zone, or something you have never done before, say yes! Learning new skills is essential to becoming a successful businessperson. You must evolve with the industry and see every new challenge as a learning opportunity. Try to say yes to everything requested unless it is dangerous, illegal, or guaranteed to lose money. You never know where the goldmine is!

Try to stay as positive as possible. Negative attitudes can bring down a business in no time. There will be challenges, and they must be dealt with, but try not to complain or let employees hear you whining. It will set the stage for their attitude. Negativity is like cancer. It grows and kills productivity and creativity.

They Take Calculated Risks

As stated before, taking risks is the key to finding new markets and opportunities. When taking a risk, be sure to weigh the potential risks and benefits beforehand. If there is a chance that you could be profitable, try it! Just be sure to put a good amount of consideration into it first. The payoff could be more than you expected! It may also be less, but the more times you try and fail, the more lessons you learn. Not everything can be taught in a book, only through experience.

Above All They Execute

Reputation is of utmost importance within a new business. You do not want to miss deadlines and get orders wrong ever, but it is especially important when you are the talk of the town! Be sure to under promise and over deliver as much as possible. Impress people with your work! Become the most reliable truck in town.

Entrepreneur Spirit is something special. Not everyone has it. In fact, a lot of people think entrepreneurs are crazy! Maybe in a way they are, but entrepreneurs have the drive to change their industry, their town or city, and the world! There are countless examples of entrepreneurs that changed the way the world works. The tech giants and department stores of the world are just a few examples. Jeff Bezos of Amazon started in his garage. Mark Zuckerberg started in his college dorm room. There is no limit to the success you can have with your business. You just have to have the right mindset, spirit, hard work, and consistency!

CHAPTER 4. BENEFITS OF OWNING A FOOD TRUCK BUSINESS

T he street food development has picked up fame in the course of the most recent couple of years, and if you've eaten from one recently, you will understand why. Street food is delightful, (typically) modest, and helpful for the client. Even TV is getting in on the act with programming highlighting road merchants in The Great Food Truck Race airing on the Food Network. If you are reading this, at that point, you are most likely keen on getting involved by beginning a mobile food business of your own. So we should investigate the main reasons why starting a 'roach coach' can be a brilliant and remunerating adventure!

Have excitement, fun, and a whole lot of road to cover and sell enthralling dishes. The idea of a food truck business is a daring one, and there are lots of benefits in starting one. Listed below are the few benefits that pop up while thinking about it:

Maneuverable on Wheels

The most vital and common benefit that comes from owning a business on wheels is maneuverability. You can travel around the country and experiment with different sites and events to put up your food truck. The best part is that whenever you decide to move, you need not "carry" all your kitchen equipment. You just have to drive with it.

Fast and Moving

Apart from maneuverability, the food truck business offers you the ability to pick up your own pace. It has all the recipes to start up a serving and dining scenario quickly. All you have to do is to drive to the desired destination and open it up for serving. With a fast and efficient moving business, you will have all the time to do the things you wanted to do—bohemian style, with a touch of class.

Cool Factor with the Taste of Assured Profit

The changes and alterations you do to your vintage van to turn it into a charming food truck is itself a perfect alluring factor to draw in curious customers. People will be ready to pay up and find out what you are offering. A cooler-looking vehicle will attract more clients who want to station your mobile pantry for service at their events. It is also a great way of investment.

Freedom to Play with the Menu

You will always have the complete freedom to change and alter the menu according to the seasonal and regional demands. Moving from place to place, you will have the versatile option of selecting from various kinds of dishes you want to serve. The refreshingly new form of business with a changing menu will bring in more customers along with the regular ones.

The comfort of Parking Anywhere You Want to

You need not worry if the customers do not come to you. With a food truck in the hold, you can drive to a busy place and start selling in an instant to a crowd. Limits are indeed low in putting up this kind of food truck. You can even put one in front of busy bars, restaurants, and retail outlets. By this, you do no harm to their business, and you can attract more people in the locality and help the ones around you along the way.

Compact Simple and Efficient Kitchen

A large kitchen is always hard to manage. Your staff will find it easier to handle the small kitchen, and he/she will be efficient in doing his/her work. Pay for your staff will also be less as they are handling a small kitchen rather than big ones.

Apart from the service, the food truck business provides similar experiences that people have in a regular restaurant. But the whole prospect of selling and buying from a mobile pantry unit is itself exciting, and this will bring in lots of benefits than you can imagine. If your dream is to cater to the hungry folks around the country in a refreshingly new way, the food truck business is apt for you to enter and have fun. Do not worry about the benefits because you are assured of getting loads of it when you are in it.

A Truck Can Go to Where the Clients Are

This may not appear that enormous of an arrangement; however, it's perhaps the greatest advantages to operating a food truck. Generally, customary cafés can only service residents that are in the encompassing zone. Accordingly, it turns out to be subject to that individual community. Moreover, there are ordinarily numerous other contending cafés in that same territory to contend with. With a mobile food business, you are not constrained to one neighborhood; you can hit a wide range of various regions, you can set up at community occasions like sporting events or festivals, attend outdoor foodie occasions or set up late-night outside of night clubs and bars. Basically, it offers you much greater flexibility as far as locations and times where you can offer food to clients.

Compared to an Independent Restaurant Overhead Expenses Are Much Lower

It is considerably less costly to set up a food truck versus setting up a new café/restaurant and all the related costs that accompany—for instance, lease, build-out, and operating expenses. Since you are regularly paying for more workers and a physical structure, your overhead costs are just that much higher.

Serving Extraordinary Food That Makes Clients Happy Will Bring a Grin to Your Face

This is maybe the most significant part of running this sort of business. A decent mobile food business can profit around $75-150,000 per year, not a huge amount of cash. But if you are serving food around an idea and menu that you have endeavored to create and truly have faith in while building relationships with the community around you, it will make the endeavor all worthwhile. Likewise, food trucks are ready for advertising via social media. The demographic of clients tends to be a more youthful, urban crowd, who are very much associated through social media. Building a loyal following through promoting and branding utilizing Facebook and Twitter is free and fun. Food trucks have been a continuous pattern for quite a long while on both the east coast and west coast (and west coast specifically because of their atmosphere), but the two coasts have garnered a youthful and dynamic crowd that have embraced food truck and road food contributions as one of a kind, trendy and vogue.

CHAPTER 5. ACQUIRING A FOOD TRUCK

There are many factors to consider when shopping for the perfect food truck that will be the backbone of your business. First of all, you'll have to consider the commercial truck restrictions within the areas that you plan on doing your day-to-day operations.

Certain cities have limits on both the length and height of commercial trucks. This may depend on crowded streets as well as parking lots. Consider that food trucks can range from 10 to 26 feet in length, while others are set up as trailer extensions.

When looking for a vehicle, just remember that you have options when it comes to obtaining a food truck. There are advantages and disadvantages to these options, but nonetheless, you need to consider all your options, especially when it comes to your budget restraints.

Renting Versus Buying

One of the choices you will likely face is deciding whether to rent or buy? This decision is entirely up to the individual food truck owner, but many experts will often suggest renting rather than buying for newcomers who have never started or run a food truck business before. With renting, new business owners will still be able to get the full experience.

With renting, newcomers will get a feel for the daily challenges that will arise from owning a food truck business. Also, renting can help newcomers learn all potential risks without forcing them to drop a heavy investment and thus putting them in a situation where there is slightly less financial risk.

To put it in perspective, purchasing a food truck can cost over $100,000 while renting can be as little as $2,000 per month, assuming the rental agreement is for at least six months. Even though your rent, keep in mind that there are also commissary costs to consider.

Buying a Food Truck

Industry experts estimate that the food truck industry will generate an astounding $2.7 billion dollars in the next few years, growing four percent in the last few years. With this in mind, truck manufacturers and outside sources have also grown with each passing year.

Among these truck manufacturers, many design and build custom trucks. When searching for a food truck designer, it's best to search for those who exist in your area; so all local regulations are met because different states require different health laws and regulations.

Truck builders should also handle all aspects of the health department approval process. This is usually a service that will make your part of the process easier. With health and safety regulations, there are extensive processes and procedures to be followed, and it's best to have a truck builder who knows how to follow these guidelines. You do not want to get this part wrong!

Exterior Design

It's astonishing how much some new mobile food business owners will spend on the interior of their food truck, only to leave the exterior less than complete. While it may feel like a waste to spend additional money on non-food related costs, the exterior is truly important.

With a food truck, it's important to understand that often only get one chance at a first impression. Within the first few seconds of seeing a mobile food truck, potential customers will immediately make the decision of whether or not they will purchase food from your truck.

Options for the exterior of a vehicle include painting or wrapping. In terms of expenses, investments for painting would cost between $1,000 and $3,000, while wrapping costs somewhere between $3,000 and $5,000, both helping to bring attention to the vehicle. However, these days, wrapping seems to be the most logical choice since almost any kind of design can be applied with a vehicle wrap.

Letters and logos should be bright, to help bring attention to your truck and hopefully attract more and more customers. The vehicle wrap acts as a billboard for your mobile business. It is actually one of the most important components of your brand. The design of your graphics can then spread to other components of your marketing, like on your website and packaging.

Be sure also to include contact information on the exterior of your vehicle. Website addresses, Facebook and Twitter IDs, are common on the sides and back panels of food trucks. Since the exterior is the most visible part of your business, you need to spend considerable time designing the look with a professional who can bring your ideas to life.

Interior Kitchen Layout

Due to the limited space, the interior kitchen layout takes planning and may need several adjustments to fit your plans in order to use the space efficiently. Especially for those building their own food truck, make sure to use every inch, making each measurement count.

Much like a contractor's advice to "measure twice and cut once," it's important to make accurate measurements when designing the interior of a food truck. If this already seems overwhelming, consider looking for a company to help with the designs. Truck builders are familiar with space restrictions and are familiar with the different types of equipment that need to be installed onto your truck.

Before purchasing any type of equipment, make sure to properly design the kitchen, creating a layout for your particular cooking style. Start by taking note of cooking procedures and even imagine where ingredients will be stored within the truck.

It's also a good idea to imagine yourself inside the truck, preparing meals at a very fast pace to get a feeling of where the bottlenecks are. The last thing you want is to find out that you placed a grill or cooler unit in the wrong spot after your truck has been delivered to you.

After deciding the necessaries for efficient operation, consider any codes that need to be followed. For example, check with local fire, health, and safety resources to determine additional necessaries, such as first aid kids or fire extinguishers that must be inside the food truck. This is why using a local truck builder can really help you to adhere to local laws and regulations for legal operation.

Everything you put into your truck takes up room. Consider the following list, and you can see that with the limited space inside a food truck, it can really fill up fast:

- Power Generator

- LED Message Board

- Custom Shelving

- Lighting

- Awnings

- Water Tank
- DVD Player, Monitors
- Service Window
- Fire Extinguisher
- Vent Hood
- Prep Table
- Air Conditioner/Heater
- Tables
- Coolers
- Propane Tanks
- Cookware
- Food Packaging
- Compartment Sink
- Refrigeration
- Cooking Equipment

Many of the above items are absolutely necessary, while others are less important. But you can see that with each service, you will need to pack everything you need to be able to serve customers without having to re-stock.

Truck Types

The two types of food trucks are lunch trucks and catering trucks. Lunch trucks are generally stainless steel catering vehicles, with one side that features a display case, while the other usually features coffee and a warming station. This is the classic "taco" truck or vending truck that you usually see at construction sites.

Catering trucks are full-service vehicles, essentially designed as a rolling kitchen. Two or three people generally operate these trucks, with one individual working with customers taking orders and collecting money while the other cooks and prepares the customer's meals.

Choosing New or Used

Used food trucks ranging anywhere from $10,000 to $75,000 are perhaps the most economical way for newcomers to purchase a "kitchen on wheels." Like purchasing any vehicle, it's a good idea to have a certified mechanic to inspect the vehicle beforehand, so you know what you're buying into.

Because the cost of a food truck is often the biggest expense, it's important to make sure that the food truck you acquire is reliable, confirming there are no unforeseen costs that may arise. In addition, new food truck owners are responsible for meeting all health requirements in their vehicles.

Even when new owners are lucky enough to find a vehicle at a great price, costs can skyrocket once you start installing all your gear.

New trucks, on the other hand, can range from $75,000 to $125,000 on average. For those who can afford it, buying new is often the ideal choice. Truck builders can provide warranties to help cover any risks that may arise within the first few years of a new purchase.

In addition, it's a good idea to speak with your builder about any other questions in regards to the food truck that you might not understand. Consider asking the builder whether or not the vehicle supplies a loaner truck (like a rental car) in case anything happens to the vehicle while it's still under warranty.

Proper Driver's License

Basically, the type of license a driver needs to operate a food truck will depend on the gross weight of the vehicle. This is the total weight of a fully-loaded truck, which includes fuel, passengers, accessories, and equipment. Depending on the truck you plan to use, a standard license will apply to anything under 26,000 pounds. That's reassuring because most food trucks weigh between 8,000 and 16,000 pounds.

If you do manage to end up with a vehicle weighing 26,000 or more pounds, a commercial driver's license or CDL is necessary. Usually, a Class B driver's license will suffice in this type of situation. A Class B license will also allow you to tow trailers that are less than 10,000 pounds. These are just simple facts, but you will need to check with your particular state to learn more about the specific requirements to avoid any possible fines for driving with the wrong type of license.

Finding the Perfect Truck

A vast cost disparity separates the simple food cart (about $2,000 USD) and a full-service food truck ($100,000). The reason for this price difference is that full-service food trucks have specialized equipment for the preparing of food, as well as selling it. With the food cart, you're equipped to sell food, but you're not equipped to compare it. Your gross profit margin will thus usually be lower with a food cart because the food you purchased wholesale is already ready for retail. Full service food trucks give the owners space and utilities to craft their own inventive cuisine fresh and on-sight, thus their profit margins are higher, and their food is fresher and better prepared, allowing them to charge more for it.

Your selection of a food truck should derive from your step 1 "concept," specifically the type of food you're preparing and the equipment and space you'll need to prepare it. The cost of your food truck will be your biggest expense, so it's important for you to take as much time as you need thinking through your preferences, your options, and the available units on the market.

For example, if you're going to be selling cupcakes primarily and doing a lot of your baking off-site, then maybe you don't need much space for cooking and preparation, but you probably should find a truck with a lot of available display area so that you can show off your enticing baked goods.

Consider buying a food truck at a lower price range of 40-60K and remodeling it to fit your concept. This is not as expensive to do as you might think and will alleviate some of the financial risks. To aid in this specific process and the food truck buying process in general, you will fare better if you can acquire the services of a competent food truck designer. Usually, companies who sell food trucks will have someone on staff who can help you with this task.

The Essentials of Designing Your Food Truck

- Making a list of all the equipment you're going to need for your particular concept.

- Obtaining the dimensions of your needed equipment.

- Determining how much overall space you will need in your food truck, both to accommodate the needed equipment and to give you and your employees enough room to operate inside the truck.

- Create a blueprint using a sheet of graph paper or a software equivalent. The blueprint will show where your equipment is placed, your display area, and where your employees will prepare the food, and where they'll interact with customers.

After you get down these basic requirements for your food truck design, an experienced food truck designer should help you polish off the details. As a warning, make sure the motivations of your designer are on the up-and-up, especially if she works for the company selling you the food truck. Your design assistant is not there to convince you to buy a larger truck or equipment that you don't need but to be a sounding board and fellow brain-stormer as you finalize your design requirements.

Your vehicle designer—though she may not be familiar with the specific state and local laws to which you're obliged—should be able to assist you in meeting basic health standards. Before you open for business, your vehicle will likely be inspected, and certain legal and health-related standards will be verified. Possible verification points include:

- Proof that you own the vehicle and that the vehicle is licensed.

- Food purchase and storage records that are up to date and accurately kept.

- Verification that you're food truck is supported by an approved and adequately equipped depot for water, general food supply, cleaning, and waste disposal.

Health department food vehicle inspections are usually conducted at once-a-year intervals and sometimes at random. Food equipment, water supplies, and sinks are all checked during these inspections. Inspections may carry over into the kitchens or garages, where the food truck is sheltered to ensure that the area is conducive to housing the truck and that fire codes are being met.

In addition to the unique inspection and licensure requirements that come from the food truck's service capacity, the truck is also subject to the standard regulations that govern every on-road vehicle, such as up-to-date registration and insurance. The motor vehicle department can clarify for you what your food truck will require in order to use the roadways. Your vehicle will probably be required to have commercial plates, though you will probably not be required to obtain a commercial driver's license to operate it so long as it's under 26,000 pounds.

When choosing where to park your food truck, you will again be subject to local ordinances. Some common local regulations include:

- **Food trucks must sell only to the sidewalk side of the street.** This prevents customers from forming a line on the street and getting in the way of traffic.

- **Food trucks must be x feet away from a bathroom at all times.** Southern California, for instance, has a rule stating that food trucks setting up for business must be within 200 feet of a bathroom if the truck is going to be parked for more than an hour.

- **Food trucks cannot park within x feet of a brick and mortar restaurant.** The tension between food trucks and traditional restaurants has gotten so high-strung in recent years that many cities have taken the role of peacekeeping into their own hands. They've done this by making compromise ordinances mandating that food trucks stay 500 to 600 feet away from established brick and mortar restaurants. In the event, these laws exist in your area of operations, make sure you get clarification on what exactly constitutes a "restaurant." Sometimes convenience stores and other non-sit-down food vendors technically count as a restaurant and are protected by the law from your competitive presence.

- **Food trucks must be parked at commissaries when they are non-operational.** Some cities are very concerned about where your food truck is going to be docked at night. Commissaries are often used as space where food truck operators can access some raw materials and prepare for their day. Even if you don't need the food-related service that a commissary provides, you still may need to rely on the commissary or another service for a space to park your vehicle when it's not in use.

- **Food trucks may only be parked on private property.** Certain municipalities have decided that food trucks in public space are just more trouble than they're worth. If you're facing these types of restrictions, then you'll need to put extra work into cultivating relationships with local businesses, office parks, etc. For a food truck, a lunch-time position in an office park, especially one that's far away from any restaurants, is an incredibly lucrative proposition.

CHAPTER 6: FOOD SAFETY

When starting a food truck business, make sure to find quality ingredients from a reputable source. Quality is generally the driving source for all customers—whether this means delicious or nutritious, quality is the key.

While cooking skills are vital, even the best chefs will find themselves coming up short when cooking with sub-par ingredients. Recipes and flavor combinations require fresh ingredients, always being the local ones a very popular choice.

Food trucks can purchase goods from various locations, including bulk stores (**Costco, Sam's Club**) or from local grocery stores. Food truck shoppers generally buy many items in bulk, just like a restaurant because of the large number of menu items needed to be prepared.

Spending less is ideal, but not when it means buying lesser quality items. Your shopping trips are most efficient when you are organized, keeping goals and accurate figures in order always to make a profit from your food.

Consider using farmer's markets and specialty shops whenever possible. It's also a good idea to state your partnerships with those markets because customers generally tend to be in-tune with supporting these sources.

Building Relationships with Suppliers

There are several fundamental reasons to build strong relationships with suppliers. Reliable suppliers are essential for any food truck business, and creating a loyal relationship will help both parties.

Suppliers can affect your food truck business in several ways. Some of these ways include quality, timeliness, innovation, finance, and competitiveness. Being rude or immoral to a supplier can quickly ruin a business, so be supportive and understanding with trusted suppliers.

You are their valued customer, so remember that you are both helping one another out. Always pay on time, giving them time to fill orders, and take the time to build a personal relationship when possible, sharing information to help both parties.

Also, as long as you feel you are fair, it is acceptable to be a demanding customer on occasion. Do not stay with a supplier that treats you unfairly or delivers products late for any inexcusable reason. Be fair, but do not be a pushover because their lack of professionalism can and will hurt your business.

Daily Operations

According to FoodSafety.gov, "forgetting about food safety is a recipe for disaster."

According to online statistics, approximately one in six Americans will get sick from food poisoning each year. These numbers become even more frightening when considering that 100,000 Americans are sent to the hospital each year for food poisoning.

Safe food handling is crucial for a food truck business. Bacteria can make people sick, and any situations like this will result in negative attitudes toward your food truck business. The following advice can help you keep customers out of harm's way.

First, make sure always to wash your hands and make sure your employees wash their hands. This is perhaps the easiest way to avoid the spread of germs.

In addition to washing your hands, make sure to clean all surfaces and utensils often. Conduct these cleanings in the most sanitary way possible, making sure to keep cleaning supplies away from ingredients.

Separate foods and never cross-contaminate. Essentially, make sure foods that are meant to be eaten raw are kept apart from ingredients like raw meat. Also, when cooking, make sure to cook all foods to their proper temperature.

Make sure all cooked foods are then properly chilled when they aren't directly served to the customer. Keep any excess in a refrigerated area in order to keep bacteria from growing.

Day-to-Day Operations

Food truck owners are generally individuals (or partners) who possess an array of skills—both managerial and functional. However, you fit in; running a successful food truck comes down to efficient day-to-day operations. Moderate and even severe challenges will always arise when you least expect it, but knowing how to handle the basics will help when difficult decisions show up.

First, make sure not to get caught up in the details, remembering to delegate whenever possible. Many new food truck owners may find themselves having trouble staying afloat because knowing how to run a food truck is not necessarily the same thing as building a successful business. There are more steps to account for when beginning a business, so that many things may become overlooked.

According to McDonald's founder, Ray Kroc, "The system is the solution." Before opening thousands of restaurants, Kroc developed a systematic approach to run the business—creating consistent, reliable, and predictable methods of operation.

Mandatory Health Inspections

With several mandatory health inspections year-round, there are various rules to follow to make sure your food truck doesn't violate any health codes. In the United States, there are over 2,000 state and local agencies responsible for keeping up with food trucks.

General regulations require food trucks to feature both hot and cold running water, a refrigerator, and a way to dispose of waste, but not each state has the same requirements. In Los Angeles, for example, food trucks must be within 200 feet of a restroom.

Currently, there are no national standards for food trucks, so it's best to evaluate the current state and local laws. Many organizations, however, believe that there will soon be a standardized list for all food trucks to follow, despite location or menu.

Like in a brick-and-mortar restaurant, health inspectors could show up just about any time to examine the cleanliness of your food truck. Make sure to sanitize frequently, cleaning all cutting boards, knives, and individual items, as well as proper food storage. It's best to follow a cleaning schedule and post procedures in visible locations so the task can be manageable. Once an inspector shows up, it's too late! You do not want to be shut down because it could really hurt your brand and reputation.

CHAPTER 7. FOOD TRUCK VEHICLE WRAPS

Your company's single most important element of physical branding is the wrap on the outside of your food truck. It immediately tells potential customers who you are and what type of business you are. This is your business' identity! It needs to be bright, colorful, and your logo should be easily readable from a distance. Your truck graphics should obviously be creative and make people interested enough to approach your truck to see what you have going on. Choosing the right graphic designer can make the difference between a good truck wrap and an awesome truck wrap.

Your food truck wrap is a very effective form of advertising, and depending on where you live; you could have 30,000 to over 60,000 people see it per day. Even when you are not open for business and serving food out of your truck, it can continue to advertise your business up to 24 hours a day as long as it is visible to the public. The wrap on your food truck can help build name recognition and overall awareness of your brand if people see it enough and associate your delicious food with the brand.

Food truck wraps can be applied in 1 to 3 days, depending on the size and square footage of the surface. If you have intricate parts on the vehicle, it can cause delays because of added difficulty in these areas. Your installer can give you fairly accurate times when they are ready to start the application process. The vinyl wrap on your truck can last five years or more depending on how you care for it. Don't use high-pressure power washers on it and avoid using anything that can scrap the vinyl. One thing you need to know as a business owner watching your budget is how long the installer will guarantee the wrap. Find out what they will do for you if the wrap starts peeling or detaching too soon. Most vehicle wraps will last longer than the time your food truck will be in business.

Make Changes to Wrap

Vehicle wraps are much more versatile than painting. I understand that in business, sometimes things change like contact information or other details. But what do you do if your phone number changes or you change your Twitter handle that is printed on your wrap? Maybe you need to make a slight change to your logo? The good news is that this type of information can be changed out quite easily on your truck even with a wrap!

The designers at the wrap company can make changes in the computer and only print out new vinyl overlays that will be applied only to the sections of your wrap that needs changing. The result is pretty seamless, and the best thing is that you don't have to pay to have the whole truck re-wrapped! The only thing you might see are edges of the newly applied sections, but even that is virtually impossible to detect unless you're looking for it.

When a change is made to a section of the wrap, it's almost as simple as applying a vinyl sticker to your truck. The installers you contract can align the new graphics, so it looks like it was original wrap. This technique can also be applied if you have a damaged section of your wrap. Your wrap installers can essentially slice out the damaged area, reprint that section and re-apply the missing vinyl and it should look as good as new.

Saving Money on Your Wrap

You want the most value for your money when it comes to your vehicle wrap. And wrapping your whole food truck can be very costly! After all, it takes a lot of vinyl to cover an entire step van. Not to mention the time needed to apply it. But what if I told you how you can potentially save money on your food truck graphics and still have a beautiful looking truck? How would that play into your marketing budget?

It may not be apparent to ordinary bystanders or even customers, but not all food trucks are completely wrapped! Some thrifty food truck owners are only applying die-cut logo decals to their trucks. This means less vinyl, less design time, less application time, and lower cost. Many food truck owners are quite happy with the results of only applying a decal of their food truck logo over the base color of their truck. Next time you're out and about, see if you can recognize the trucks that have a full wrap vs just decals. I think you'll be surprised how many are not fully wrapped. However, I've seen my fair share of trucks that feature beautiful full color wraps that catch my attention every time!

If you proceed with only adding a logo or minor graphics to your truck, please be sure that the underlying surface of the vehicle is clean and attractive. What I mean is that you don't want to have a lot of noticeable scratches, rust, dents, and other distractions on the exterior of your truck. You want your graphics to be applied to clean and smooth surfaces that help enhance your graphics or logo. Positioning is important. Will it still be visible when you have the side panels open? If not, will you have a logo on another spot on the truck that will remain visible even if your main graphic is not?

You can even have phone numbers, website addresses, social media contact information, and other details produced in vinyl that are adhered to the exterior panels of your truck. These can be smaller pieces of vinyl that have your business information on them. You can significantly reduce the time it takes to apply graphics to your truck if it is not a complete wrap. Utilize the existing exterior color of your truck if you can. However, most trucks are probably white or grey in color, but that can provide a nice clean background for your graphics to stand out.

If the color of your truck is important for your overall branding, you could have it painted a solid color and then use separate vinyl graphics around the exterior of your truck. Obviously, if you decide to paint your food truck, your overall costs will go up.

The Production Process

Wrap companies are dedicated to working with you to come up with the best designs that fit within your requirements. They often have in-house designers who can work one-on-one with you to create the exact look you want. You should be able to see your design come together throughout the design phase. You should request previews during the design stage and whenever there are changes. Be sure to voice your concerns or requests during this process to save time back-tracking. Your designer will thank you for it!

When the designs are finished, your designer should send you mock-ups, explanations, and the final proof before the design is sent off for printing. You should approve or suggest changes before it goes to print. The time to make modifications is while the design is still on the computer. Otherwise, you can incur more expenses.

When your graphics are ready for printing, most wrap companies will have their own large-format printers in their warehouse. Before printing, take a look at examples of previous wraps they have done. Look at the finish of the wrap and see if there are any options you forgot before you actually have them print. If all looks good, then give them the green light to start the printing process.

Wrap companies often have their own facilities where they wrap vehicles. Often it'll be a warehouse or large garage because they have to accommodate vehicles of various sizes. Sometimes they might rent or share an existing warehouse with another company so they can keep their overhead lower.

Something to keep in mind is that you may have to travel to get your wrap applied to your truck. You may live in a city that doesn't have a wrap installer. If that's the case, you will have to bring your food truck to them in order for them to work on your vehicle. It could be several hundred miles away or even in the next state! But keep in mind that you do not have to be in the same city as the wrap company for the design phase. All of that can be worked on over the phone and online.

If you have windows on your truck, the wrap company can also wrap the windows. But keep in mind that they will not apply vinyl to the front windshield or the front side windows. If you choose to have them wrap any of the other windows, see if they can use perforated vinyl so you can still see out those windows. This is especially important for rear windows. From the outside, the design will still look seamless, but from the inside of the vehicle, you will still be able to see out but it is impaired a bit. An example of this would be like on a city transit bus. You know the ones that have been completely wrapped like a moving billboard? Everything is covered on the bus, including the windows.

To a bystander, all the text, graphics and images look pretty seamless on the exterior of the bus. But on the inside, passengers can still see out the windows through the thousands of little dots punched into the vinyl in the window sections. It's like looking through a fly screen except denser.

How to Know I've found The Best Food Truck Business

Not every person who offers a feast in a hurry is in a similar class. To find the right portable food truck business, you need to do some examination. Do you need a concession business like the one on each other corner? Or on the other hand, would you like to be the food concession that offers a crisp and one of a kind menu that stands in a class independent from anyone else?

You start a new business for yourself since you need to turn a benefit. To do that, you need to choose your activity shrewdly. A decent portable food truck system will provide all the fundamental devices, assets, and guidance to guarantee that you escape the door rapidly and effectively. Giving this a shot your very own will prompt many stumbles and wrong turns. Do you believe you have room schedule-wise and cash to hazard going only it? So before settling on anything, find an industry leader who has a training program set up and systems intended to spare you long periods of experimentation.

The best versatile food businesses have a demonstrated business model that is constructed and intended to pull in customers from a large fragment of the populace. They provide you with training from the day you consent to your Franchise Arrangement and support for whatever length of time that you are in business.

Where lunch customers once needed to agree to solidified level, boring burgers, solidified fries, and sandwiches with a couple of choices, the best versatile food concessions offered hand-tapped Vermont meat burgers and healthy options, for example, an assortment of new wraps. They have developed exponentially every year and keep on outperforming desires even in a horrid economy.

When you choose to band together with the top versatile concession establishments, you will maintain a portable food business with heart. You and your staff will have an extraordinary time serving customers with a full menu of exciting and healthy choices. Furthermore, when you're working in a kept space, there's no space for error. Your training gives all of you the plans and food preparation protocols that you need to attract into your customer base and surpass their desires every single visit. What's more, their best in class electronic announcing systems and back-office support means you never need to manage long stretches of desk work.

CHAPTER 8. PROS AND CONS OF THE FOOD TRUCK LIFESTYLE

The food trucker lifestyle isn't exactly for everyone. If you're going to venture into this kind of business, then you have to be prepared to be very hands-on, since food businesses, in general, need complete supervision, especially for startups. To further determine whether a food truck business is for you, let's go through the pros and cons so that you can weigh each aspect and make a decision as to whether you'd want to pursue the venture or not.

Pros of Opening a Food Truck Business

Low Overhead Investments

As mentioned earlier, opening a food truck business requires relatively low overhead costs to start up as compared to a restaurant. All you need is a truck, a kitchen, equipment, inventory, and extra money for maintenance and gas. The rest can be spent on marketing and advertising. For the truck, you can actually rent food trucks for a fixed rate and add your own design as long as your decorations and art can be taken off. In fact, that is what you should do to test your concept and a truck you are considering buying before shelling out big cash. More about that later.

It is cheaper in the long run to buy your own truck, but for those who are low on budget, renting can be a good startup option. You also need a kitchen, sometimes called a commissary where food is prepared, prior to the business day. These are available for rent, but in the beginning, unless there is a need for commercial equipment, it is best to use your own kitchen. Why a kitchen? Newbies to the food truck business sometimes believe that food prep can easily be handled in the truck or on a cook to order basis.

First, the operation of food truck kitchen equipment is much more expensive than your own kitchen, whether it be propane for gas, or an electric generator fueled by gasoline on the truck. Second, a key to your success will be the speed at which you can serve each item on your menu. Thoughtful prep should be used in every possible way to reduce cooking and serving times. Long lines of people waiting on food will drive away customers.

Very successful food truck businesses evolve to a point where there is a prep team and sometimes even a runner who is constantly delivering pre-cut veggies or extra supplies of sliced meat, etc.

You will need kitchen equipment and supplies for preparing the food (e.g., stove, pots, pans, etc.).

Easy to Get Customers

As compared to the regular food establishments, food trucks will usually go to their customers and not the other way around. For a typical restaurant, the establishment will wait for the customers to come. In the food business, there are peak hours and dead hours, with peak hours being the time with the most customers (usually during lunch and dinner time) and dead hours wherein there are little to no customers (usually after lunch or late afternoon when everyone is in the office).

The great thing about food trucks is that during dead hours, they can go around and look for business because they're mobile anyway, or they can use this time to prep for the next busy time, using a reduced staff. Your business won't have waiters sitting around waiting for a single late diner and a manager overseeing them.

If the area where they're in doesn't have customers, they can look for another area with a lot of people or call it a day. This opens up many opportunities for developing your business through marketing and other important planning. This is also a great strategy to get the words out about your business, getting you more potential customers in the long run.

Easy for Catering

If you offer catering, then things will be easier for you. You don't need to hire delivery to ship all the food to the destination since you can just use your food truck. You can store all of your food in the food truck and preserve it properly while still bringing a product that is top quality because it didn't "sit" in a heater waiting to be served. You may even tie up with catering companies, who would want to make use of your truck for serving customers when you are not running. The opportunities in the catering industry are ripe and wide. This should definitely be an early focus on growing revenue.

Easy for Participating in Events

Food trucks can easily access in festivals or other public events and get more customers. If a certain event (like a carnival) is happening, you can tie-up with the organizers of the carnival to grab a good spot there and just park in a well-located area serving tons of people. In fact, you don't even need to tie up with organizers at an event sometimes.

You can just park your truck right outside the event, and the people will come to your truck. For instance, if there happens to be a concert, you can just park your truck near the entrance (if the organizers allow it). There are hundreds of people in line waiting to get in who are hungry or thirsty. You can take advantage of that kind of situation.

Cons of a Food Truck Business

This is Still a Risky Business

This business, done right, is still going to require upfront outlay of material cash. Later, we will provide ideas for reducing these costs and testing your concept to avoid a massive cash failure, but like all businesses, a number of food trucks do fail. Well planned trucks with good concepts thrive, so that is what we must be.

Tough to Manage Inventory

One of the main disadvantages of having a food truck is that it is tough to manage inventory. Let's say that you've got a really good business day, and customers finished up all your food inventory. If it's in the middle of the day and you still want to continue serving food, you either have to go back to your kitchen or get someone to deliver. On slower days, food can be wasted if customers are not there. This is why tracking sales, both to location and on a per-event basis, is critical to managing your food costs.

Vague Regulations for Food Truck Businesses

Unlike regular restaurants, regulations for food truck businesses in some areas can be quite vague. There is a temptation to skirt regulations or shortcut certifications, but DO NOT do this. Health regulators regularly check food trucks, especially where they are gathered together in groups, and you do not want to deal with a shutdown at a critical time and the major fines associated with failing to comply. The good news is that the growth of the food truck industry is causing local officials to make it easier to get the information necessary to be in compliance. Some cities already give food truck owners very clear guidelines on how to operate. Be sure to study the laws and regulations regarding food truck businesses in your area before venturing forward. We are working on a tool that will assist here, but the importance of accurate up to date information cannot be understated.

Competition

There is a vast competition in this industry. As the trend of the food truck business gains momentum, more and more people are interested in the idea. The critical way to overcome this challenge is to have an exceptional product and an innovative brand. Creativity with marketing, and hard work to get your truck in high traffic areas as frequently as possible, will have you blowing past the competition quickly.

CHAPTER 9. CUSTOMER PROGRAMS

Getting new customers is the way you grow your business. It's no wonder that businesses exert a lot of time and money to bring in new customers. Studies have shown that it costs 5 to 10 times more to acquire a new customer than it does to sell to a loyal existing customer. There's also research that reveals that existing customers spend 67% more than new customers. So, you can see that keeping customers coming back is extremely beneficial to your food truck business. The mobile food industry is very competitive, so you need to attract and keep customers, so they'll buy from you and not your competitors.

So, what can you do to keep your customers coming back and spending their money with you? The answer is with a customer loyalty program. A good portion of businesses have implemented some sort of customer loyalty or rewards program to entice customers to come back and buy.

American Airlines was one of the first to implement a customer loyalty program on a large scale and was the first program that was widely accepted in the United States. The idea was to give their passengers something special for flying with them. This was the first frequent flyer program that allowed passengers to accrue miles to use on future flights as long as they continued to fly on American Airlines. Today, frequent flyer programs are commonplace in the airline industry.

Loyalty programs work the best with businesses that serve repeat customers. Restaurants and food trucks fall into that category. If you have amazing food and great customer service, you will get repeat customers. To keep them coming back, reward them for their continued patronage. How many times have you visited a restaurant to get that 11th sandwich for free?

Effective Loyalty Programs

You've probably seen a loyalty program in many businesses you've visited. But a loyalty program is simply a rewards program that companies offer to customers that make frequent purchases. This loyalty program rewards customers who keep coming back with special offers, gifts, free merchandise, coupons, and more!

While loyalty programs seem like it's simple to implement, let me throw out the following facts. A recent study has shown that a given household typically has memberships to 29 loyalty programs. However, only out of all those they have signed up for, they are really only engaged in about 12 of them. That means a lot of companies and spending a lot of time and money on rewards programs but seeing very little to no benefit from them. The key is to offer value to your customers for being a part of your loyalty program. So how do you increase your ability to make loyalty programs be more effective for your food truck business?

Loyalty Program Features

Loyalty programs are offered by many companies, and the choices can be overwhelming. Some are simple, while others are feature-rich and advanced. It's important to pick one that you think will work with your food truck business for the long term. However, you can never tell if these loyalty programs will close shop or be acquired by a larger rewards program. But you can't let that fear stop you from implementing a loyalty program.

I will give you some ideas and suggestions when searching for a loyalty program that is right for you. Use this as a guide so you can be better informed before you implement a system for your food truck. It is not uncommon to switch programs if, over time, you find that it is not working for you. Here are some suggestions and features to consider.

Simple Point Systems

One of the most common and oldest loyalty program systems is the point system. Customers that visit your food truck frequently can accrue points that can be redeemed for rewards once they've reached the threshold you've set. They can receive a discount, free items or even special treatment and more!

You've seen these before, and can come in many forms. Some are simple punch cards, while others use magnetic cards and a database to keep track of points. The point system should be simple to understand. Don't over-complicate this! The term points can refer to various tracking methods. For example:

Buy 10 sandwiches get the 11th free.

Spend $50 get your next dish free.

The point system encourages frequent short-term purchases that keep customers coming back, accruing points, and eventually getting rewarded for their continued visits to your food truck. You can assign points by the number of items or by the dollar amount spent.

Tier System

There is a tricky balance between a loyalty program and offering desirable rewards that are attainable. You don't want to create a huge process in order for customers to reach reward thresholds. That will turn off your customers, and your loyalty system becomes ineffective. One way to breach this problem is to use a tier system.

With a tier system, you can offer a reward for initially joining your loyalty program. This encourages sign-ups. Then you can bring back returning customers by increasing the value of the rewards you offer in different tiers. Each tier is made more attractive by offering higher value or better rewards as they move up the ladder. This can help customers remember your loyalty program because it encourages decreasing the time it takes for them to redeem their rewards. If the time between payouts for the reward is too long, customers will forget or ignore the loyalty program. The biggest difference between a points system and a tier system is that customers receive their rewards in the short-term.

So with your food truck business, you can offer a free appetizer or drink for the initial sign up to your loyalty program. Then after that, you can offer larger and larger rewards such as two appetizers free when they reach the next tier and then offer something else in subsequent tiers.

How to Measure Effectiveness

Just because you've implemented your loyalty program it doesn't mean you're done! You need to be able to measure the success of your efforts. The goal of your loyalty program is to increase your customer's satisfaction and keep them coming back.

In today's business world, you will most likely be using a rewards program with an online database. These systems offer excellent tracking and analytics. A punch card system can work, but it will be much more difficult to evaluate its effectiveness.

Customer Retention Rate

When evaluating your analytics, you want to first look at your Customer Retention Rate. This is a measurement of how long your customers continue to buy from you. If your loyalty program is successful, this number should increase over time as you continue to add people to your program. Studies have shown that even a 5%

increase in customer retention can translate to a 25% to 100% increase in your company's profits.

Negative Churn

You may or may not have heard the term churn. But churn is the rate that your customers stop doing business with you. When I say negative churn, it indicates the rate at which customers increase spending with you. Negative churn helps to balance out the natural occurrence where customers leave your business.

Net Promoter Score

The net promoter score is based on customer satisfaction and how likely they are to recommend your business to others. This is usually on a scale of 1 to 10, with 10 being the highest. The net promoter score is calculated by taking the percentage of detractors (people who wouldn't promote your business) and subtracting it from the number of promoters (people who would recommend your business).

The fewer detractors you have, the better. You can consider a net promoter score of 70% and higher a good number, and having a great loyalty program can help you reach that number. To get the satisfaction rating, you will have to send out surveys to customers. These are usually based online and can be sent as notifications via your chosen loyalty program.

When to Implement a Loyalty Program

Loyalty programs can be implemented at any time during your business. For some older businesses, they've been doing business for years before starting a loyalty program. That could be because reliable systems weren't available when they started, and now they realize the benefits of having it.

Others start a loyalty program from the beginning or early on. But here's a suggestion. If you haven't launched your food truck yet, get on board with a loyalty company that fits for your business.

Have it in place before you launch. Then when you launch your truck, you can start customers on your loyalty program right from the start. Hold a special event when you launch.

If you cater to events, this is also a great place to gather multiple signups in one location. When you're at a catering event, guests have more time to spend with you and your business. Keep in mind any events where you have to opportunity to sell your loyalty program.

Here is a shortlist to get you started. These companies can come and go, so by the time you read this, some of them may or may not be in business anymore.

- Belly

- Square

- LevelUp

- FiveStars

- Wali

- Perka

- SpotOn

- PunchCard

- SpendGo

- Swipley

- FourSquare

Most, if not all, the rewards systems listed above utilize mobile apps and digital tracking to make it easy for your customers to keep track of their reward status. This helps customers know when they are close to receiving a reward and could entice them to come back for a visit.

Choosing Rewards for Customers

The kind of rewards offered to customers varies depending on the type of business. But there are some general rules to follow that increase the chances of a positive reward experience for your customers. Experts advise expanding your thinking from only offering discounts on your goods. That's because the discounts don't have a long-lasting impact on customer's impressions. Rewards that have physical items are received and remembered much better than a plain discount. Luckily in the food truck industry, we can talk straight to customer's stomachs!

A good way to tailor your own rewards program is to imitate larger successful programs from related companies and offering something unique. You can research brick-and-mortar restaurants, bakeries, ice cream shops, food trucks and more to see what they are doing. Sign up for their programs so you can see first-hand how theirs works and to see the types of rewards they offer. Ask yourself if they seem reasonable and if their rewards are something that would even interest you.

Put together a program that offers the best of what you've seen and experienced. Another factor that determines how your rewards program works is tied directly to the service that you sign up for. Some have more features than others. You may or may not need certain features. Price and fees will also be a factor. Weed out the ones that don't fit your budget or have features you don't need or will never use. In the end, your customers want to be able to reap the rewards. It is ideal for them to be able to redeem an award about every 3 to 6 months, so they don't forget about it. This will help stimulate them to come back and buy. A loyalty program should not take too long for a customer to see the results of their continued business with you. Otherwise they will see no value in it.

It's a well-known fact that loyalty programs are a very effective marketing tool. When successfully implemented, they can help increase profits and keep customers coming back for more. Loyalty programs can also help boost your brand awareness and, ultimately, your reputation. If you haven't done so, start researching the different loyalty programs available and plan out how you would implement them into your business. You don't want to be missing out on an excellent marketing opportunity that can result in a lot of positive advantages for your food truck!

Learn How to Get Client's Buying from Your Food Truck

Breakfast 5:30-11:30 am Timing All You Need

In the event that your food truck will work during morning hours, offering cooking intended for morning foods would clearly be important. Although expensive, a grinder ($1500) and coffee espresso system (over $3500) would be a delightful addition to the truck. In any case, would you say you are making a piece of art with your truck or a business? Try not to lose sight who is going to your truck for his/her "morning joe." In the event that they needed a $4 double coffee, they'd almost certainly go to a cafe and sit down. Then again, don't ration the quality of coffee you use. You should offer a choice of crisply blended gentle to medium coffee, a solid mix, and a decaf mix (A decent machine should run about 500USD.).

Everything with eggs is lovely, and if you need to get crepes, fancier, and waffles is an extraordinary expansion. Be that as it may, it would be ideal if you keep it basic to your benefit. Morning clients are by and large in a rush, so you can't take too long to even think about preparing.

Baked products from your preferred local baker are the ideal accessories to offer with your hot foods. Care ought to be taken with respect to who you buy these baked products. Here as well, don't get excessively detailed; clients need to eat and run.

The greater part of anything you need to serve hot for a morning meal fare can be set up on a blistering level top griddle. That leaves a lot of space for other hardware that can be utilized for prep of your lunch and supper cooking styles. "Little things create daily propensities," so by keeping your morning food basic, simple-to-serve and modest, you can expect a one time fulfilled clients to stop by your truck the following day... And the next...

Lunch 11:30-5:30pm, Dinner 5:00-11:00pm

Now things get intriguing here. Hot dogs, pizzas, and hamburgers are available all over the place. It is preferable to be unique and creative in the design of your dinner and lunch fare. The dependable guideline doesn't change such a great amount from that of the morning cooking styles, which means your client needs something quick, scrumptious, and sensibly valued. Do a food that isn't found in the region in which you need to work. What's more, don't think about stopping too close to an existing café or restaurant! You'll make an adversary forever; also, the official or city authority may come down to you too. But, location is an alternate story, which I will write about at another point. In the event that your clients need to lounge around sitting tight for their order, they should sit serenely in an eatery. Keep your costs reasonable and ideally lower than neighborhood eateries with the goal that your food truck transforms into an increasingly wanted spot to go as well.

CHAPTER 10. FOODS YOU CAN GET STARTED WITH

Most popular food truck meals are barbeque, burgers, Pizza, Cupcakes, Grilled Cheese, Lobster Rolls, and roll fried snails, but what matters most is understanding what your customers want and what sells most in that vicinity.

Butternut Squash Hummus

Preparation time: 5 Minutes

Cooking time: 30 Minutes

Servings: 4

Ingredients:

- 2 Pounds butternut squash, seeded and peeled

- 1 Tablespoon olive oil

- ¼ Cup tahini

- 2 Tablespoons lemon juice

- 2 Cloves of garlic, minced

- Salt and pepper to taste

Directions:

1. Heat the oven to 3000F.

2. Coat the butternut squash with olive oil.

3. Place in a baking dish and bake for 15 minutes in the oven.

4. Once the squash is cooked, place in a food processor together with the rest of the ingredients.

5. Pulse until smooth.

6. Place in individual containers.

7. Put a label and store it in the fridge.

8. Allow warming at room temperature before heating in the microwave oven.

9. Serve with carrots or celery sticks.

Nutrition:

Calories per serving: 115; Carbs: 15.8g; Protein: 2.5g; Fat: 5.8g; Fiber: 6.7g

Cheesy Olives Bread

Preparation time: 10 minutes

Cooking time: 30 minutes

Servings: 10

Ingredients:

- 4 Cups whole-wheat flour

- 3 Tablespoons oregano, chopped

- 2 Teaspoons dry yeast

- ¼ Cup olive oil

- 1 and ½ Cups black olives, pitted and sliced

- 1 Cup water

- ½ Cup feta cheese, crumbled

Directions:

1. In a bowl, mix the flour with the water, the yeast, and the oil, stir and knead your dough very well.

2. Put the dough in a bowl, cover with plastic wrap, and keep in a warm place for 1 hour.

3. Divide the dough into 2 bowls and stretch each ball really well.

4. Add the rest of the ingredients to each ball and tuck them inside well kneading the dough again.

5. Flatten the balls a bit and leave them aside for 40 minutes more.

6. Transfer the balls to a baking sheet lined with parchment paper, make a small slit in each, and bake at 425 degrees F for 30 minutes.

7. Serve the bread as a Mediterranean breakfast.

Nutrition:

Calories 251; Fat 7.3g; Fiber 2.1g; Carbs 39.7; Protein 6.7g

Flax Meal Porridge

Preparation time: 5 Minutes

Cooking time: 30 Minutes

Servings: 4

Ingredients:

- 2 Tablespoons sesame seeds

- ½ Teaspoon vanilla extract

- 1 Tablespoon butter

- 1 Tablespoon liquid Stevia

- 3 Tablespoons flax meal

- 1 Cup almond milk

- 4 Tablespoons chia seeds

Directions:

1. Preheat your air fryer to 375°Fahrenheit.

2. Put the sesame seeds, chia seeds, almond milk, flax meal, liquid Stevia, and butter into the air fryer basket tray.

3. Add the vanilla extract and cook porridge for 8-minutes.

4. When the porridge is cooked, stir it carefully, then allow it to rest for 5-minutes before serving.

Nutrition:

Calories: 298; Total Fat: 26.7g; Carbs: 13.3g; Protein: 6.2g

Scrambled Pancake Hash

Preparation time: 5 Minutes

Cooking time: 30 Minutes

Servings: 4

Ingredients:

- 1 Egg

- ¼ Cup heavy cream

- 5 Tablespoons butter

- 1 Cup coconut flour

- 1 Teaspoon ground ginger

- 1 Teaspoon salt

- 1 Tablespoon apple cider vinegar

- 1 Teaspoon baking soda

Directions:

1. Combine the salt, baking soda, ground ginger, and flour in a mixing bowl.

2. In a separate bowl crack, the egg into it.

3. Add butter and heavy cream.

4. Mix well using a hand mixer.

5. Combine the liquid and dry mixtures and stir until smooth.

6. Preheat your air fryer to 400°Fahrenheit.

7. Pour the pancake mixture into the air fryer basket tray.

8. Cook the pancake hash for 4-minutes. After this, scramble the pancake hash well and continue to cook for another 5-minutes more.

9. When the dish is cooked, transfer it to serving plates, and serve hot!

Nutrition:

Calories: 178; Total Fat: 13.3g; Carbs: 10.7g; Protein: 4.4g

Greek Couscous Salad and Herbed Lamb Chops

Preparation time: 5 Minutes

Cooking time: 30 Minutes

Servings: 4

Ingredients:

- ¼ Tsp salt

- ½ Cup crumbled feta

- ½ Cup whole wheat couscous

- 1 Cup water

- 1 Medium cucumber, peeled and chopped

- 1 Tbsp finely chopped fresh parsley

- 1 Tbsp minced garlic

- 2 ½ lbs. Lamb loin chops, trimmed of fat

- 2 Medium tomatoes, chopped

- 2 Tbsp finely chopped fresh dill

- 2 Tsp extra virgin olive oil

- 3 Tbsp lemon juice

Directions:

1) On medium saucepan, add water and bring to a boil.

2) In a small bowl, mix salt, parsley, and garlic. Rub onto lamb chops.

3) On medium-high fire, place a large nonstick saucepan and heat oil.

4) Pan-fry lamb chops for 5 minutes per side or to desired doneness. Once done, turn off the fire and keep warm.

5) On saucepan of boiling water, add couscous. Once boiling, lower fire to a simmer, cover, and cook for two minutes.

6) After two minutes, turn off the fire, cover, and let it stand for 5 minutes.

7) Fluff couscous with a fork and place into a medium bowl.

8) Add dill, lemon juice, feta, cucumber, and tomatoes in the bowl of couscous and toss well to combine.

9) Serve lamb chops with a side of couscous and enjoy.

Nutrition:

Calories per Serving: 524.1; Carbs: 12.3g; Protein: 61.8g; Fat: 25.3g

Paprika Chicken and Pineapple Mix

Preparation time: 10 minutes

Cooking time: 30 minutes

Servings: 4

Ingredients:

- 2 Cups pineapple, peeled and cubed

- 2 Tablespoons olive oil

- 1 Tablespoon smoked paprika

- 2 Pounds chicken breasts, skinless, boneless, and cubed

- A Pinch of salt and black pepper

- 1 Tablespoon chives, chopped

Directions:

1. Heat up a pan with the oil over medium-high heat, add the chicken, salt and pepper, and brown for 4 minutes on each side.

2. Add the rest of the ingredients, toss, cook for 7 minutes more, divide everything between plates, and serve with a side salad.

Nutrition:

Calories 264; Fat 13.2g; Fiber 8.3g; Carbs 25.1g; Protein 15.4g

Ginger Garlic Pork Ribs

Preparation time: 5 Minutes

Cooking time: 30 Minutes

Servings: 4

Ingredients:

- 1lb. Baby pork ribs
- 1 Tablespoon olive oil
- 1 Tablespoon hoisin sauce
- ½ Tablespoon honey
- ½ Tablespoon soy sauce
- 3 Garlic cloves, minced

Directions:

1. In a bowl, add the ingredients and mix well.

2. Place the marinated ribs in the fridge for 2-hours. Place marinated ribs in the air fryer basket at 320°Fahrenheit for 40-minutes.

Nutrition:

Calories: 287; Total Fat: 12.5g; Carbs: 11.5g; Protein: 16.2g

Creamy Curry Salmon

Preparation time: 10 minutes

Cooking time: 30 minutes

Servings: 2

Ingredients:

- 2 Salmon fillets, boneless and cubed
- 1 Tablespoon olive oil
- 1 Tablespoon basil, chopped
- 1 Cup Greek yogurt
- 2 Teaspoons curry powder
- 1 Garlic clove, minced
- ½ Teaspoon mint, chopped

- Sea salt and black pepper to the taste

Directions:

1. Heat up a pan with the oil over medium-high heat, add the salmon and cook for 3 minutes.

2. Add the rest of the ingredients, toss, cook for 15 minutes more, divide between plates and serve.

Nutrition:

Calories 284; Fat 14.1g; Fiber 8.5g; Carbs 26.7g; Protein 31.4g

Smoked Salmon and Veggies Mix

Preparation time: 10 minutes

Cooking time: 30 minutes

Servings: 4

Ingredients:

- 3 Red onions, cut into wedges

- ¾ Cup green olives, pitted and halved

- 3 Red bell peppers, roughly chopped

- ½ Teaspoon smoked paprika

- 3 Tablespoons olive oil

- 4 Salmon fillets, skinless and boneless

- 2 Tablespoons chives, chopped

- Salt and black pepper to the taste

Directions:

1. In a roasting pan, combine the salmon with the onions and the rest of the ingredients, introduce in the oven and bake at 390 degrees F for 20 minutes.

2. Divide the mix between plates and serve.

Nutrition:

Calories 301; Fat 5.9; Fiber 11.9; Carbs 26.4; Protein 22.4

Salmon and Mango Mix

Preparation time: 10 minutes

Cooking time: 30 minutes

Servings: 2

Ingredients:

- 2 Salmon fillets, skinless and boneless

- Salt and pepper to the taste

- 2 Tablespoons olive oil

- 2 Garlic cloves, minced

- 2 Mangos, peeled and cubed

- 1 Red chili, chopped

- 1 Small piece ginger, grated

- Juice of 1 lime

- 1 tablespoon cilantro, chopped

Directions:

1. In a roasting pan, combine the salmon with the oil, garlic, and the rest of the ingredients except the cilantro, toss, introduce in the oven at 350 degrees F and bake for 25 minutes.

2. Divide everything between plates and serve with the cilantro sprinkled on top.

Nutrition:

Calories 251; Fat 15.9; Fiber 5.9; Carbs 26.4; Protein 12.4

Spanish Rice Casserole with Cheesy Beef

Preparation time: 5 Minutes

Cooking time: 30 Minutes

Servings: 4

Ingredients:

- 2 Tablespoons chopped green bell pepper

- 1/4 Teaspoon Worcestershire sauce

- 1/4 Teaspoon ground cumin

- 1/4 Cup shredded Cheddar cheese

- 1/4 Cup finely chopped onion

- 1/4 Cup chile sauce

- 1/3 Cup uncooked long grain rice

- 1/2-pound Lean ground beef

- 1/2 Teaspoon salt

- 1/2 Teaspoon brown sugar

- 1/2 Pinch ground black pepper

- 1/2 Cup water

- 1/2 (14.5 ounce) Can canned tomatoes

- 1 Tablespoon chopped fresh cilantro

Directions:

1. Place a nonstick saucepan on medium fire and brown beef for 10 minutes while crumbling beef. Discard fat.

2. Stir in pepper, Worcestershire sauce, cumin, brown sugar, salt, chile sauce, rice, water, tomatoes, green bell pepper, and onion. Mix well and cook for 10 minutes until blended and a bit tender.

3. Transfer to an ovenproof casserole and press down firmly. Sprinkle cheese on top and cook for 7 minutes at 400oF preheated oven. Broil for 3 minutes until the top is lightly browned.

4. Serve and enjoy with chopped cilantro.

Nutrition:

Calories per serving: 460; Carbohydrates: 35.8g; Protein: 37.8g; Fat: 17.9g

Tasty Lasagna Rolls

Preparation time: 5 Minutes

Cooking time: 30 Minutes

Servings: 4

Ingredients:

- ¼ Tsp crushed red pepper

- ¼ Tsp salt

- ½ Cup shredded mozzarella cheese

- ½ Cups parmesan cheese, shredded

- 1 14-oz Package tofu, cubed

- 1 25-oz Can of low-sodium marinara sauce

- 1 Tbsp Extra virgin olive oil

- 12 Whole wheat lasagna noodles

- 2 Tbsp Kalamata olives, chopped

- 3 Cloves minced garlic

- 3 Cups spinach, chopped

Directions:

1. Put enough water on a large pot and cook the lasagna noodles according to package instructions. Drain, rinse, and set aside until ready to use.

2. In a large skillet, sauté garlic over medium heat for 20 seconds. Add the tofu and spinach and cook until the spinach wilts. Transfer this mixture to a bowl and add parmesan olives, salt, red pepper, and 2/3 cup of the marinara sauce.

3. In a pan, spread a cup of marinara sauce on the bottom. To make the rolls, place noodles on a surface and spread ¼ cup of the tofu filling. Roll up and place it on the pan with the marinara sauce. Do this procedure until all lasagna noodles are rolled.

4. Place the pan over high heat and bring to a simmer. Reduce the heat to medium and let it cook for three more minutes. Sprinkle mozzarella cheese and let the cheese melt for two minutes. Serve hot.

Nutrition:

Calories per Serving: 304; Carbs: 39.2g; Protein: 23g; Fat: 19.2g

Tortellini Salad with Broccoli

Preparation time: 5 Minutes

Cooking time: 30 Minutes

Servings: 4

Ingredients:

- 1 Red onion, chopped finely
- 1 Cup sunflower seeds
- 1 Cup raisins
- 3 Heads fresh broccoli, cut into florets
- 2 Tsp cider vinegar
- ½ Cup white sugar
- ½ Cup mayonnaise

- 20-oz Fresh cheese-filled tortellini

Directions:

1. In a large pot of boiling water, cook tortellini according to manufacturer's instructions. Drain and rinse with cold water and set aside.

2. Whisk vinegar, sugar, and mayonnaise to create your salad dressing.

3. Mix together in a large bowl red onion, sunflower seeds, raisins, tortellini, and broccoli. Pour dressing and toss to coat.

4. Serve and enjoy.

Nutrition:

Calories per Serving: 272; Carbs: 38.7g; Protein: 5.0g; Fat: 8.1g

Lemon Rainbow Trout

Preparation time: 10 minutes

Cooking time: 30 minutes

Servings: 2

Ingredients:

- 2 Rainbow trout

- Juice of 1 lemon

- 3 Tablespoons olive oil

- 4 Garlic cloves, minced

- A pinch of salt and black pepper

Directions:

1. Line a baking sheet with parchment paper, add the fish, and the rest of the ingredients and rub.

2. Bake at 400 degrees F for 15 minutes, divide between plates and serve with a side salad.

Nutrition:

Calories 521; Fat 29g; Fiber 5g; Carbs 14g; Protein 52g

Banana-Coconut Breakfast

Preparation time: 5 Minutes

Cooking time: 30 Minutes

Servings: 4

Ingredients:

- 1 Ripe banana
- 1 Cup desiccated coconut
- 1 Cup coconut milk
- 3 Tablespoons raisins, chopped
- 2 Tablespoon ground flax seed
- 1 Teaspoon vanilla
- A dash of cinnamon
- A dash of nutmeg
- Salt to taste

Directions:

1. Place all ingredients in a deep pan.

2. Allow it to simmer for 3 minutes on low heat.

3. Place in individual containers.

4. Put a label and store it in the fridge.

5. Allow it to thaw at room temperature before heating in the microwave oven.

Nutrition:

Calories per serving: 279; Carbs: 25.46g; Protein: 6.4g; Fat: 0g; Fiber: 5.9g

Morning Time Sausages

Preparation time: 5 Minutes

Cooking time: 30 Minutes

Servings: 4

Ingredients:

- 7 Ounces ground chicken

- 7 Ounces ground pork

- 1 Teaspoon ground coriander

- 1 Teaspoon basil, dried

- ½ Teaspoon nutmeg

- 1 Teaspoon olive oil

- 1 Teaspoon minced garlic

- 1 Tablespoon coconut flour

- 1 Egg

- 1 Teaspoon soy sauce

- 1 Teaspoon sea salt

- ½ Teaspoon ground black pepper

Directions:

1. Combine the ground pork, chicken, soy sauce, ground black pepper, garlic, basil, coriander, nutmeg, sea salt, and egg. Add the coconut flour and mix the mixture well to combine.

2. Preheat your air fryer to 360°Fahrenheit. Make medium-sized sausages with the ground meat mixture.

3. Spray the inside of the air fryer basket tray with the olive oil. Place prepared sausages into the air fryer basket and place inside of the air fryer.

4. Cook the sausages for 6-minutes. Turn the sausages over and cook for 6-minutes more. When cooking time is completed, let the sausages chill for a little bit. Serve warm.

Nutrition:

Calories: 156; Total Fat: 7.5g; Carbs: 1.3g; Protein: 20.2g

Baked Bacon Egg Cups

Preparation time: 5 Minutes

Cooking time: 30 Minutes

Servings: 4

Ingredients:

- 2 Eggs

- 1 Tablespoon chives, fresh, chopped

- ½ Teaspoon paprika

- ½ Teaspoon cayenne pepper

- 3-ounces Cheddar cheese, shredded

- ½ Teaspoon butter

- ¼ Teaspoon salt

- 4-ounces Bacon, cut into tiny pieces

Directions:

1. Slice bacon into tiny pieces and sprinkle it with cayenne pepper, salt, and paprika.

2. Mix the chopped bacon.

3. Spread butter in the bottom of ramekin dishes and beat the eggs there.

4. Add the chives and shredded cheese.

5. Add the chopped bacon over the egg mixture in ramekin dishes.

6. Place the ramekins in your air fryer basket. Preheat your air fryer to 360°Fahrenheit.

7. Place the air fryer basket in your air fryer and cook for 12-minutes.

8. When cooking time is completed, remove the ramekins from air fryer and serve warm.

Nutrition:

Calories: 553; Total Fat: 43.3g; Carbs: 2.3g; Protein: 37.3g

Coconut Yogurt

Preparation time: 5 Minutes

Cooking time: 30 Minutes

Servings: 4

Ingredients:

- 1 Tablespoon Gelatin

- 3 Cups Coconut Cream

- 1 Package Yogurt Starter

Directions:

1. Start by adding in your coconut cream to your instant pot before pressing the yogurt setting.

2. Remove the pot and turn it off.

3. Allow it to cool in the fridge for ten minutes before moving onto the next step.

4. Afterward, stir in your yogurt starter until it's smooth, and put your pot back into your instant pot.

5. Press your yogurt button again, setting the time to eight hours. Stir in your gelatin gradually.

6. Refrigerate for at least four hours before serving.

Nutrition:

Calories: 421; Protein: 5.6g; Fat: 42.9g; Carbs: 10.2g; Sodium: 32mg

Tasty Beef and Broccoli

Preparation time: 5 Minutes

Cooking time: 30 Minutes

Servings: 4

Ingredients:

- 1 and ½ Pounds flanks steak, cut into thin strips
- 1 Tablespoon olive oil
- 1 Tablespoon tamari sauce
- 1 Cup beef stock
- 1 Pound broccoli, florets separated

Directions:

1. In a bowl, mix steak strips with oil and tamari, toss and leave aside for 10 minutes.

2. Set your instant pot on sauté mode, add beef strips, and brown them for 4 minutes on each side.

3. Add stock, stir, cover pot again, and cook on high for 8 minutes.

4. Add broccoli, stir, cover pot again, and cook on high for 4 minutes more.

5. Divide everything between plates and serve.

6. Enjoy!

Nutrition:

Calories: 312; Protein: 4g; Fat: 5g; Carbohydrates: 20g

Beef Corn Chili

Preparation time: 5 Minutes

Cooking time: 30 Minutes

Servings: 4

Ingredients:

- 2 Small onions, chopped (finely)
- ¼ Cup canned corn
- 1 Tablespoon oil
- 10 ounces Lean ground beef
- 2 Small chili peppers, diced

Directions:

1. Take your instant pot and place over a dry kitchen surface; open its top lid and switch it on.

2. Press. "SAUTE."

3. In the Cooking pot, add and heat the oil.

4. Add the onions, chili pepper, and beef; cook for 2-3 minutes until turn translucent and softened.

5. Add the 3 water cups to the Cooking pot; combine to mix well.

6. Close its top lid and make sure that its valve is closed to avoid spilling.

7. Press "MEAT/STEW." Adjust the timer to 20 minutes.

8. Press will slowly build up; let the added ingredients to cook until the timer indicates zero.

9. Press "CANCEL." Now press "NPR" for natural release pressure. Instant pot will gradually release pressure for about 8-10 minutes.

10. Open the top lid; transfer the cooked recipe to serving plates.

11. Serve the recipe warm.

Nutrition:

Calories: 94; Protein: 7g; Fat: 5g; Carbohydrates: 2g

Balsamic Beef Dish

Preparation time: 5 Minutes

Cooking time: 30 Minutes

Servings: 4

Ingredients:

- 3 pounds Chuck roast
- 3 Cloves garlic, thinly sliced
- 1 Tablespoon oil
- 1 Teaspoon flavored vinegar
- ½ Teaspoon pepper

- ½ Teaspoon rosemary

- 1 Tablespoon butter

- ½ Teaspoon thyme

- ¼ Cup balsamic vinegar

- 1 Cup beef broth

Directions:

1. Cut slits in the roast and stuff garlic slices all over.

2. Take a bowl and add flavored vinegar, rosemary, pepper, thyme, and rub the mixture over the roast.

3. Set your pot to sauté mode and add oil; allow the oil to heat up.

4. Add roast and brown both sides (5 minutes each side).

5. Take the roast out and keep it on the side.

6. Add butter, broth, balsamic vinegar and deglaze the pot.

7. Transfer the roast back and lock up the lid; cook on HIGH pressure for 40 minutes.

8. Perform a quick release.

9. Remove the lid and serve!

Nutrition:

Calories: 393; Protein: 37g; Fat: 15g; Carbohydrates: 25g

Soy Sauce Beef Roast

Preparation time: 5 Minutes

Cooking time: 30 Minutes

Servings: 4

Ingredients:

- ½ Teaspoon beef bouillon
- 1 ½ Teaspoon rosemary
- ½ Teaspoon minced garlic
- 2 Pounds roast beef
- 1/3 Cup soy sauce

Directions:

1. Mix the soy sauce, bouillon, rosemary, and garlic together in a mixing bowl.

2. Place your instant pot over a dry kitchen platform. Open the top lid and plug it on.

3. Add the roast, bowl mix, and enough water to cover the roast; gently stir to mix well.

4. Properly close the top lid; make sure that the safety valve is properly locked.

5. Press "MEAT/STEW" Cooking function; set pressure level to "HIGH" and set the cooking time to 35 minutes.

6. Allow the pressure to build to cook the ingredients.

7. After cooking time is over, press the "CANCEL" setting. Find and press the "NPR" Cooking function. This setting is for the natural release of inside pressure, and it takes around 10 minutes to release pressure slowly.

8. Slowly open the lid, take out the cooked meat and shred it.

9. Add the shredded meat back in the potting mix and stir to mix well.

10. Take out the cooked recipe in serving containers. Serve warm.

Nutrition:

Calories: 423; Protein: 21g; Fat: 14g; Carbohydrates: 12g

Almond Butter Cookies

Preparation time: 5 Minutes

Cooking time: 30 Minutes

Servings: 4

Ingredients:

- ½ Cup slivered almonds
- 1 Stick butter, room temperature
- 2 Tablespoons Truvia
- 1/3 Cup almond flour

- 1/3 Cup coconut flour

- 1/3 Teaspoons ground cloves

- 1 Tablespoon candied ginger

- ¾ Teaspoon pure vanilla extract

Directions:

1. In a mixing dish, beat Truvia, butter, vanilla extract, ground cloves, and ginger until light and fluffy. Then, throw in both kinds of flour and slivered almonds.

2. Continue to mix until a soft dough is formed.

3. Cover and place into the fridge for 35-minutes. Preheat your air-fryer to 315°Fahrenheit.

4. Roll the dough into small cookies and place them on the air-fryer cake pan; gently press each cookie using the back of a spoon.

5. Bake cookies for 13-minutes.

Nutrition:

Calories: 252; Total Fat: 16.2g; Carbs: 25.1g; Protein: 3.3g

Chocolate Raspberry Cake

Preparation time: 5 Minutes

Cooking time: 30 Minutes

Servings: 4

Ingredients:

- 1/8 Teaspoon fine sea salt

- 1 Tablespoon candied ginger

- ½ Teaspoon ground cinnamon

- 2 Tablespoons cocoa powder

- 3-ounces Almond flour

- 1 Egg plus 1 egg white, lightly whisked

- ¼ Cup unsalted butter, room temperature

- 2 Tablespoons Truvia for baking

For Filling:

- 6-ounces Raspberries, fresh

- 1 Tablespoon Truvia

- 1 Teaspoon lime juice, fresh

Directions:

1. Preheat your air-fryer to 315°Fahrenheit. Then, spritz the inside of two cakes pans with buttered-flavored cooking spray. In a mixing bowl, beat Truvia and butter until creamy. Then, stir in the whisked eggs. Stir in the cocoa powder, flour, cinnamon, ginger, and salt. Press the batter dividing it evenly into cake pans; use a wide spatula to level the surface of the batter. Bake for 20-minutes.

2. While your cake is baking, stir together the ingredients for filling in a saucepan. Cook over high heat, stirring often and mashing; bring to a boil and decrease the temperature. Cook for about 7-minutes or until mixture thickens. Allow filling to cool at room temperature.

3. Spread half of the raspberry filling over first cake, then top with other cake, and spread the remaining raspberry filling on top.

Nutrition:

Calories: 331, Total Fat: 14.9g, Carbs: 47.6g, Protein: 26.9g

Papaya Cream

Preparation time: 10 minutes

Cooking time: 0 minutes

Servings: 2

Ingredients:

- 1 Cup papaya, peeled and chopped

- 1 Cup heavy cream

- 1 Tablespoon stevia

- ½ Teaspoon vanilla extract

Directions:

In a blender, combine the cream with the papaya and the other ingredients, pulse well, divide into cups and serve cold.

Nutrition:

Calories 182; Fat 3.1g; Fiber 2.3g; Carbs 3.5g; Protein 2g

Almonds and Oats Pudding

Preparation time: 10 minutes

Cooking time: 30 minutes

Servings: 4

Ingredients:

- 1 tablespoon lemon juice

- Zest of 1 lime

- 1 and ½ Cups almond milk

- 1 Teaspoon almond extract

- ½ Cup oats

- 2 Tablespoons stevia

- ½ Cup silver almonds, chopped

Directions:

1. In a pan, combine the almond milk with the lime zest and the other ingredients, whisk, bring to a simmer and cook over medium heat for 15 minutes.

2. Divide the mix into bowls and serve cold.

Nutrition:

Calories 174; Fat 12.1; Fiber 3.2; Carbs 3.9; Protein 4.8

Date & Hazelnut Cookies

Preparation time: 5 Minutes

Cooking time: 30 Minutes

Servings: 4

Ingredients:

- 3 Tablespoons sugar-free maple syrup

- 1/3 Cup dated, dried

- ¼ Cup hazelnuts, chopped

- 1 Stick butter, room temperature

- ½ Cup almond flour

- ½ Cup cornflour

- 2 Tablespoons Truvia for baking

- ½ Teaspoon vanilla extract

- 1/3 Teaspoon ground cinnamon

- ½ Teaspoon cardamom

Directions:

Firstly, cream the butter with Truvia and maple syrup until the mixture is fluffy. Sift both types of flour into bowl with butter mixture. Add remaining ingredients. Now, knead the mixture to form a dough; place in the fridge for 20-minutes.

To finish, shape the chilled dough into bite-size balls; arrange them on a baking dish and flatten balls with the back of a spoon. Bake the cookies for 20-minutes at 310°Fahrenheit.

Nutrition:

Calories: 187; Total Fat: 10.5g; Carbs: 23.2g; Protein: 1.5g

Orange and Apricots Cake

Preparation time: 10 minutes

Cooking time: 30 minutes

Servings: 8

Ingredients:

- ¾ Cup stevia
- 2 Cups almond flour
- ¼ Cup olive oil
- ½ Cup almond milk
- 1 Teaspoon baking powder
- 2 Eggs
- ½ Teaspoon vanilla extract

- Juice and zest of 2 oranges

- 2 Cups apricots, chopped

Directions:

1. In a bowl, mix the stevia with the flour and the rest of the ingredients, whisk and pour into a cake pan lined with parchment paper.

2. Introduce in the oven at 375 degrees F, bake for 20 minutes, cool down, slice, and serve.

Nutrition:

Calories 221; Fat 8.3g; Fiber 3.4g; Carbs 14.5g; Protein 5g

Blueberry Cake

Preparation time: 10 minutes

Cooking time: 30 minutes

Servings: 6

Ingredients:

- 2 Cups almond flour
- 3 Cups blueberries
- 1 Cup walnuts, chopped
- 3 Tablespoons stevia
- 1 Teaspoon vanilla extract
- 2 Eggs, whisked
- 2 Tablespoons avocado oil
- 1 Teaspoon baking powder
- Cooking spray

Directions:

1. In a bowl, combine the flour with the blueberries, walnuts, and the other ingredients except for the cooking spray, and stir well.

2. Grease a cake pan with the cooking spray, pour the cake mix inside, introduce everything in the oven at 350 degrees F and bake for 30 minutes.

3. Cool the cake down, slice, and serve.

Nutrition:

Calories 225; Fat 9g; Fiber 4.5g; Carbs 10.2g; Protein 4.5g

Blueberry Yogurt Mousse

Preparation time: 30 minutes

Cooking time: 0 minutes

Servings: 4

Ingredients:

- 2 Cups Greek yogurt
- ¼ Cup stevia
- ¾ Cup heavy cream
- 2 Cups blueberries

Directions:

1. In a blender, combine the yogurt with the other ingredients, pulse well, divide into cups and keep in the fridge for 30 minutes before serving.

Nutrition:

Calories 141; Fat 4.7g; Fiber 4.7g; Carbs 8.3g; Protein 0.8g

Nutmeg Lemon Pudding

Preparation time: 10 minutes

Cooking time: 30 minutes

Servings: 6

Ingredients:

- 2 Tablespoons lemon marmalade

- 4 Eggs, whisked

- 2 Tablespoons stevia

- 3 Cups almond milk

- 4 Allspice berries, crushed

- ¼ Teaspoon nutmeg, grated

Directions:

2. In a bowl, mix the lemon marmalade with the eggs and the other ingredients and whisk well.

3. Divide the mix into ramekins, introduce in the oven, and bake at 350 degrees F for 20 minutes.

4. Serve cold.

Nutrition:

Calories 220; Fat 6.6g; Fiber 3.4g; Carbs 12.4g; Protein 3.4g

CHAPTER 11. PLAN YOUR MENU

What's Easy for You to Cook

Can you cook hotdogs without burning either side? Can you flip pancakes like a pro? Do you know how to make delicious patties with just the right amount of condiments? You have to determine what you can cook so you can narrow your choices down instead of overwhelming yourself with the thought that you should cook every dish in the world.

Find Your Specialty

Of course, there are a couple of dishes that you know how to cook, and that's exactly why you're planning to open a food truck business. But there will always be a dish that you're confident about and that you know you can cook better than anyone else does. What is it? Think about it and think about how you can use it for this business. For example, you can cook Fettuccine Alfredo like you're from Italy, and you know that it tastes different from what others make. Think about that and see if you can make more variations or if you want to feature the said dish with some side dishes. This way, when people think about your food truck, they'll remember your specialty dish, and they'd keep coming back for more.

Ingredients That Are Easy to Get Around You

Maybe, you're planning to put up a hotdog food truck but you're in an area where there's loads of fish and fresh produce around. What do you do? Will you still get meat for the hotdog from another town? or will you make use of the ingredients close to you, especially if you can actually make great dishes out of them. Sometimes, it's important to look around and see what you can do with what you have around you because that will save you a lot of money and may even make you closer to people around you, as well!

What the People Around You Love to Eat or What They Look For

Get to know your customers. Of course, it may be impossible to meet each and every one of them, but it wouldn't be impossible to observe and make a general assessment as to what kind of food they enjoy the most. This way, when you set up your food truck, you can be sure that at least one or two people will try what you have to offer. On the other hand, you can also observe what's lacking in the area, and you can check whether you can give them that or not. For example, New York is full of these pizza, pretzel, and hotdog kiosks, and food trucks. However, there's a lack of sushi trucks or even trucks that sell ramen or maybe even something organic. You see, there are so many things that you can cook and offer people, so research on that. If you offer people what they're missing or what's not currently available in the area, you just might get a positive response because, more often than not, people want to try what they still haven't before.

Ingredients Are Too Costly

Think about the dishes that you'll be making and see to it that you're not wasting too much money on ingredients, especially if you don't have enough budget, to begin with. Think about a dish that you can make, and you know you're good at that won't cost too much. It's important not to waste a lot of money when you're only starting.

Portable Ingredients

There may be times when you lack ingredients in the truck, and you have to buy some more from the nearest store—but what if it's a couple of miles away? You have to think about the ingredients that you'll be using, too, because they're important when it comes to the dishes that you'll be cooking.

Food Products That Are Easy to Re-Heat

If you're planning to set up an Industrial Catering Vehicle, it would be important to know which food products can you easily re-heat without them losing their quality, and you have to learn which foods don't get spoiled easily, as well, as you'll be traveling around a lot.

Focus on Your Expertise or Try Something New

Suppose you're famous for creating delicious and appetizing cupcakes. Are you going to sell them or make them the focus of your business? Or are you also willing to learn how to make other dishes and make use of them, too? Diversity is very important when it comes to food trucks, sure, but being confident with what you're doing is also one of the biggest keys to success.

Your Menu Always Be Your Menu or You Will Be Able to Change It

It's important to observe whether your customers like your menu or not and be open to changes if needed.

The Time You Will Be Open and on Which Days

You have to create a schedule, and you have to stick to it because when your customers notice that you're not around for a day or two, and when they feel like you're not open at a certain given time, they may think that you're no longer in business or that you're not serious with what you're doing—and that's definitely something that you shouldn't allow to happen.

Make Sure That You Are Consistent

Consistent in what, you ask? Well, consistent when it comes to making good food. Remember that you're not planning to have people eat at your place and never come back anymore, right? So, you have to make sure that you always get to create good food so when they recommend you to other people, they won't be embarrassed that they did so and you'd gain more customers, too.

Extras

As time goes by, you can also add more dishes to your menu, and you may also add some other items in your truck that you could sell. These items include official merchandise with the name of your business, some souvenirs that customers can give away, and other things that will remind them of your business so that they won't forget it right away. Make sure though that you leave them a good impression so they'd want to buy these extra items.

If you know how to plan your food truck menu, things will definitely be much easier for you!

Pro Tips

A Larger Menu Does Not Equal Larger Sales

Edit yourself during this stage of developing your food business. You can always add to your menu after you establish a loyal following. Start simple. Get good at what you are doing, then add. Wendy's first menu was burgers, chili, fries, sodas, and chocolate Frostys. Now they have a variety of chicken, salads, baked potatoes, and different flavored Frostys. Follow their original example; your patience and bank account will thank you.

It is time to go back to the computer and research a few questions about street food in your area.

By this point, you should be aware of any regulations or restrictions that could limit your menu or serving daypart. (breakfast, lunch, dinner, snack, late-night are dayparts in restaurant lingo)

The research includes & will be a part of your business plan:

What is missing in the street vending scene in my town?

What is currently being sold that I already have a superior recipe for?

What are the current prices in my area for common street foods? (like soda, chips, hot dog, hamburger, tacos, etc.)

Who is a weak link in the street vending? (poor reviews, low health inspection scores, spotty service, inconsistent operating hours)

What would I love to sell?

What foods am I already good at?

Where can I source the ingredients for my food?

Will my menu excite people and encourage them to buy?

What cooking equipment will I need for my menu? (flat top griddle, char-broiler, fryer, wok, pressure cooker, etc.)

How will cooked foods be held?

What serving/portioning utensils will be needed?

Testing Should Happen After You Make the Decision to Begin a Food Business and Before You Order Equipment

Testing products is paramount. If possible, test the products on folks that will give honest feedback. Rely on co-workers, church members, PTA members, high school sports teams anyone other than friends and family.

The reason is simple: you may discover either your recipe is not well received or your local economy can't/won't support the prices you have to charge to be profitable.

Create an anonymous survey asking for feedback. You will need this feedback to improve your food. Set upon a sliding scale (rank 1 to 5), sample questions could include:

The food is served hot and fresh

The quality of food

The food is tasty and flavorful

A proper amount of sauces and condiments

If this product were priced at $XX.XX would you consider it too low, too high, or exactly right?

Are the condiment portions a good value for the proposed price?

Is the price would be competitive with other food trucks

Please provide any other feedback you may have

Of the foods served today, which was your favorite?

Keep the survey around ten questions. The longer the questionnaire, the less likely you are to get valuable feedback as the participant will rush answering.

Where to Find Your Food Supplies

Once you are confident with the recipe and ingredient portions, you should begin searching for high-quality yet affordable sources for all your food and paper products. Quality, availability, and pricing are the important parts of this step.

Vendors are often challenged with minimum orders or having a set location to accept delivery when looking at large national distributors like **Sysco, GFS, Chaney Brothers, or US Foods**. Often local and regional distributors are more flexible when dealing with a mobile vendor. Contact every supplier that runs routes to your town. They may be able to assist your business. You could also partner with other vendors (that don't compete directly with your menu) to get the case count up to the minimum. Many distributors will contact you with driver delivery times so you can meet at your commissary to accept your food order.

Other sources are **Sam's Club, Costco, Restaurant Depot, Webstaurantstore.com, BJ's** or local wholesale bakeries, butchers, and produce companies.

Again, using computer research food distributors in your area. You may be surprised how many you didn't even know about.

Category	Source	ingredient	measure	case size	cost	portion cost
Bread	Sams	Hamburger Bun	Each	24	$ 3.48	$ 0.15
Condiments	Sams	Ketchup	ounce	114	$ 3.83	$ 0.03
Condiments	Sams	Mayo	ounce	128	$ 6.98	$ 0.05
Condiments	Sams	Mustard	ounce	105	$ 4.28	$ 0.04
Condiments	Sams	Pickles	Each	300	$ 4.92	$ 0.02
Dairy	Sams	American Cheese	Slice	120	$ 10.58	$ 0.09
Meat	Sams	Hamburgers	Each	40	$ 24.98	$ 0.62
Paper	Sams	#6 bags	Each	500	$ 18.64	$ 0.04
Paper	Sams	15x15 wrap	Each	3000	$ 81.86	$ 0.03
Paper	Sams	gloves	Each	100	$ 2.98	$ 0.03
Paper	Sams	Napkins	Each	3000	$ 13.57	$ 0.00
Produce	City Product	SHREDDED LETTUCE 5#	ounce	5	$ 5.37	$ 1.07
Produce	City Product	TOMATO 5 by 6	each	30	$ 16.00	$ 0.53
Produce	Sams	Red Onions	Lbs	1	$ 0.98	$ 0.98
						$ -

In the spreadsheet, you will notice I list the category the ingredient falls in, where I buy it from, the name of the ingredient, how the product will be portioned, how many is in a case, what the case costs, and how much a portion will cost.

If you look at the 'source' column, you will notice only two different sources for the burger ingredients. Sam's Club and City Produce (a local production company in Fort Walton Beach).

You should shop around looking for the best products and the best pricing. Don't be afraid to have several suppliers for your ingredients. Also, source a backup distributor; you never know when your main supplier will be out or run short.

Pricing Your Menu

Pricing your menu properly can be scary, especially if you have never sold anything. Assigning a fair value to products can be difficult for some people.

Make prices too low, and you may be quite busy but have little to show for it.

Go too high, and no one stops to eat. In pricing, you have to be Goldilocks, finding that "just right" balance of price vs. value.

Value goes beyond high quality products on your menu. Value is perceived in the delivery of said menu. Clean cart or trailer, fantastic service, witty interaction with your guests, location convenience, all play a part in adding value to your products.

How many times have you groaned at the price of toilet paper at a convenience store only to buy it anyway because it saved you time? Your location provides a food choice for your guests plus saving them time, gasoline, and trouble.

The point of difference in your food service business must be in the overall Guest Experience you provide. What is that, you ask?

There Are Four Elements That Define a Food Service Operation No Matter the Size Service Style or Sales Volume

Quality

Pertains to high standards (freshness, taste, temperature, smell, etc.) yet profitable ingredients. Finished products presented with care and respect. Attention to food detail, such as neat assembly, uniformity of hand-cut items, today's portions are exactly the same as last weeks and next weeks, etc.

Quality, pertaining to food, means buying the best, fresh wholesome ingredients you can profitably afford and then preparing them in a safe manner that respects the ingredient. Finally, assembling and presenting a delicious tasting, neatly assembled product to the guest. In other words: keep hot food hot, cold food cold, and chips crispy.

Service

Fast and friendly, courteous, respectful, and inviting attitude. More attention to details verifying the served food meets quality standards and is going to the right person. Smiles, speed, and personality win every time.

Cleanliness

Of course, is sparkling, sanitary conditions in your cart, trailer, or truck. Cleanliness also applies to the area surrounding your setup, your organizational skills in the kitchen, and neat, tidy areas guests may use like condiment tables.

Community

Being a part of your community – a good neighbor- if you will. It is the emotional connection your guests have towards your business. Location convenience, involvement in the local community, fundraising, going the extra mile for a special request, providing more than required at catered events. Restaurant commercials you see on TV that DON'T mention food usually are tugging at your heart creating an emotional connection to the brand.

CHAPTER 12. MARKETING YOUR TRUCK

M arketing really starts with learning about your customer and what they want to buy. You may have a concept for your food truck, but long before you launch or finalize your menu, you need to talk to potential customers and test, test, test! These early tests can be used determine the viability of your concept, theme, menu, ingredients, attitude, and more!

If your marketing strategy is off, no amount of advertising or PR can fix it. There are many ways to market a business or service. Most businesses share common marketing tactics, while others have more unique ways of carrying out a marketing plan.

In today's business environment, marketing can take on very creative forms. And there are so many tools we can use and so many channels to market our businesses. Marketing can be a simple paper flyer that is photocopied and handed directly to people, or it can be much more involved with major planning and elaborate productions. There are no hard-set rules when it comes to marketing. Creativity and research often are key factors when it comes to a successful marketing plan.

Some of us have very creative plans for how to deliver messages to current and potential customers. There are some people who just have a natural ability to come up with ideas that help promote business. But some of us struggle when it comes to marketing, and that's when you need to decide if you're going to assign that role to someone else. Look to your partner or staff members for ideas.

Who knows? You may have a marketing genius already working for you! In some cases, you may need to hire a marketing specialist to create a successful marketing plan for you. Yes, this adds an extra expense to your food truck business, but the added cost can be well worth the expense in the long run.

There are many parts to marketing a food truck business but they all work together to help grow your business. Some of the strategies are long-term, while some can be quick little promotions scheduled around special events and holidays. A lot of it will be online through social media while some of it is more tangible on a day-to-day basis.

Facebook

Facebook can be a powerful marketing tool to help you get more customers if you know how to use it effectively. Facebook can have incredible reach with the right type of audience. Some of the statistics for Facebook users are incredible, and it continues to astound researchers. There are 1.3 billion active users on Facebook, with 680 million of those users connecting on mobile devices. And users aged 18-34 are quite active, with 48% of them checking Facebook as soon as they wake up, racking up an average of 18 minutes per session! So you can see that if you do not already have a Facebook page for your food truck, you need to start one right now!

How to Get More Engagement

One of the things you can do to increase engagement from your fans is to post content more often. The number of times you post may depend on your schedule but I suggest 5-7 postings per week is a good amount to let your fans know you are active on your page. A Facebook page that is perceived to be active with you interacting with your followers is more likely to have engaged fans that will actually pay attention to your updates.

An easy way to post Facebook updates is to share interesting photos and videos from an exciting day of business. These are better than just text-based posts because people love to skim their timeline, and posts with an image or video usually attracts more attention. The more attention, the more Likes you can potentially get.

With an image post, in the beginning, you might get 1 like out of it. This may happen to most of your image postings. You may not get any likes from your image and get frustrated with this process. This often discourages a lot of people trying to build a following on Facebook. But if you can put aside those feelings and continue to post on a regular schedule, you will eventually find the one post that will start the momentum going.

But the popularity can vary depending on the quality of what you are sharing with your audience. You need to be able to gauge what your followers want to know about from your business. Experts tell us that fans want posts that are quick and easy to read because, as you know, everybody is busy, and most people want to skim headlines to get their info. But not only do your posts have to be brief, but they also have to have certain qualities to attract them, like educating them about you or your product, entertain them in some way, or even enlightening them. Let me explain these three items in a bit more detail in the context of food truck marketing.

Educational Posts: Just like the title says, this type of posting should teach your fans something that can really benefit them. It could be your special technique of frying French fries to the perfect crispness or even the best way to marinate meat for the most intense flavor. You have skills that others want to learn.

Entertaining Posts: These types of posts can be about almost anything. But one of the main things is that it has to be able to attract and keep the reader's attention. These can be quirky or funny posts. If you have an exceptionally busy day, you can post a video of how crazy the kitchen can be when there seems to be no end to the customer line outside.

You might want to mount a couple of GoPro cameras inside and outside your truck to capture anything interesting happening. This footage will have to be edited down before posting, but it's a good way to have a camera around without it getting in the way of your cooking.

In the food truck industry, you can include some of these ideas in your postings:

- Food images

- Ingredient images

- Food truck images

- Shots of the team cooking

- Your location or venue

- Photos of special guests

- Special events you are attending

- Shots of your truck at unique landmarks

- Close-ups of food from the interior of your truck

- Cooking equipment

- Daily menu specials

- Signature dishes

- Behind the scenes photos

- Impromptu photos during a service

- Shots of new products or menu items

- Ingredient shopping trips

- Mechanical issues

How to Find Time to Post on Facebook

Posting to Facebook at least once a day can sound like a challenging task when you are juggling the seemingly endless to-do list of your daily operations. This is where your mobile phone comes in handy. Whenever you're working on your food truck, just remember to take out your phone or tablet and snap a picture or shoot a short video when you see something that would be fun for your followers.

You can even have your staff members do the same. Make them part of your marketing efforts. If they have a smartphone, instruct your staff also to take photos or videos that would be worthy of posting on Facebook. Some owners don't want their employees to have access to the company's Facebook account, and that is understandable. A simple solution to that is to have them send you their media to your phone, so you can do it yourself.

The problem is that you still need to find time to upload a post during a busy day. So I'm going to introduce you to a technique called "batching" that is utilized by many entrepreneurs to be as productive as possible.

What Batch Posting Is

Batching is where you lump together similar tasks into one session instead of stringing it out over the course of a day. Batching also helps you focus on the task at hand so you can do a better job at it. Not only does this get you in the zone, but it can also save you time.

A good example of batching can be found when checking and responding to emails. Email is constantly being fed to our Inbox, and reading and responding to emails each time an alert comes up is not an efficient use of time. The solution for busy people is to batch the email process. This means not reading or responding to emails at the time they come in. Instead, set a time during the day where you can sit down for maybe half an hour and be dedicated to just email-related tasks. At your set time, go through all your emails and respond to those senders that need attention. If you get a lot of emails, you might set a time to check them in the middle of the day and then again in the evening.

This is just one example of batching, but it can be applied to lots of related tasks. Shopping for ingredients and prepping your food are other examples of batching that are used in the food truck industry.

How Batching Apply to Facebook

You might be wondering how you are going to apply the technique of batching on Facebook? Luckily for us, Facebook allows users the ability to schedule posts. This is a huge benefit for food truck owners. Now you don't have to take a timeout during a busy service to post something to Facebook.

Using Facebook scheduling, you can now prepare and write posts weeks in advance. This means you can have a week's worth or more posts ready to go live automatically exactly when you want your followers to see them.

You can now strategically set posts to go live as you are about to open for business without having to log into Facebook at the time you're preparing for your service. You'll find the scheduler by clicking on the down arrow next to the *Publish* button. You'll be presented with a dropdown menu. Simply choose *Schedule Post,* then select the time and date you want the post to be published. Write your post and attach any photos or video to it and then click *Schedule*. Now repeat that process until you have banked several posts into the queue. You have successfully batched this task, and now your posts will automatically go live at the times you've set.

Posts That Can Be Repeated

So now that we know how to batch posts on Facebook, I want to talk about posts you should schedule on a regular basis. Now your food truck has a schedule, and for the most part, you are at many of the same locations on a weekly basis. The Facebook scheduler can be an excellent tool to automatically let your fans know where you're going to be on a given day.

One type of posting you should include in your batching sessions are the locations where you'll park at for the following week. You could even schedule these location posts for an entire month if you want. Most food truck owners know where they're going to be parked in the current month or even further out. Just schedule your posts half an hour to an hour before you arrive at your location. This will give your followers time to see your announcement and get to your location. You have now automated one of your marketing tasks!

When people visit your Facebook page, the first thing they're going to see is your cover photo. Visitors can't miss it because it's the largest image at the top of the screen. It almost covers the whole width of the Facebook window. You want something compelling and unique for this image! This image should shout out what your food truck is all about!

Maybe you could insert a photo of your truck if you have some stunning graphics to show off. Another idea would be to put a clean version of your logo there... but there's a better place for your logo, as we'll explain later. Lastly, you could insert a beautiful image of one of your signature dishes to make people hungry when they visit your page. Just remember that this main image should spark some sort of reaction or make an impression with your visitors.

Email Marketing

For years, successful marketers have used email to help promote products, companies, events, and more! Email marketing is an extremely effective way to get your message directly to your customers. However, in the past, some abused this strategy, and thus, the term Spam was born. Even with this tarnished reputation, email marketing still remains a viable and cost-effective way to reach customers.

When I say cost-effective, you'll have to realize that good email marketing services are not free, like Twitter and Facebook. But it does offer opportunities that the free social media tools don't have. I know you might be saying, "Why should I spend money on email marketing when I can use Twitter and Facebook for free?"

Website

Your website is an essential element of your marketing plan. If you don't have a website these days, you're missing out on the ability to let customers get information about you 24 hours a day. Businesses can spend a decent part of their startup budget on a web designer. But if you haven't hired a designer to build your website yet, I would suggest that you build it yourself!

That's right! Build it yourself! Don't worry if you don't have any coding skills. It's easier to do than you think! Lots of technically challenged people are starting their own websites with WordPress. WordPress is a free content management system that has changed the way websites are built and maintained. Originally designed for blogging, WordPress has evolved to become the standard management platform for a large percentage of websites on the internet today. It is available for free on all hosting plans that offer it.

Pinterest for Food Trucks

In early 2012, there were a reported 5 million users on Pinterest, with nearly 1.5 million unique visitors daily. Those users spent at least 15 minutes per day on the site. Another stunning fact is that Pinterest drove more traffic to websites than LinkedIn, Google+, YouTube, and Reddit combined!

A few businesses might have a hard time finding a connection with Pinterest if there aren't very many visual elements tied to their business but food trucks can definitely take advantage of this popular network.

Before you start pinning images, you should think about the names of different "Boards" you want your images to appear in. A board is basically a category or folder where you will organize your images. Pinterest users can follow one of your boards or all. For Cheez Philly, I could create the following boards:

- Cheez Philly

- Food Truck Graphics

- Street Food

- Cheesesteak

- Gourmet Sandwiches

- San Diego Food Truck

- Yum

You don't have to create all your boards at once, but you should come up with creative names that draw attention. When you pin a photo, you are allowed to include a description. Be detailed when you add your text.

YouTube Marketing

Online video has become a large part of how our society gathers information and be entertained. One of the largest and most popular video sharing sites is YouTube, with 300 minutes of video is uploaded per minute every day. YouTube has helped simplify the task of sharing video to the masses by hosting user videos for zero cost.

YouTube is not only a great business promotion tool, but when leveraged correctly, you can also build trust and recognition for your company. It may not seem like it at first, but YouTube is really an elaborate and sophisticated social network. Because of the simplicity of YouTube's interface, uploaded videos can be spread to other social sharing platforms, including Facebook,

Twitter, your own website, blog and even in email communications. YouTube videos can spread quickly if they become popular or go viral. So for food trucks, if you are already using social media, you definitely should be incorporating YouTube into your overall marketing strategy.

Give a Tour of Your Food Truck

Many businesses, large and small, use YouTube video marketing to introduce customers to their products and services. Food truck owners are lucky in that there are a lot of visual opportunities that can be captured on camera. Your truck itself can provide a nice backdrop and used as a subtle branding cue if you are standing in front of your truck. Food trucks are always on the go and parked in various locations. A walk around your truck can make for an interesting video.

If you are still in the building phase of your truck, it makes perfect sense to capture footage during the process so you can share it with your future customers. Get them excited about your launch. It's never too early to start marketing your business. Not only do customers get to see how your food truck is coming along, but you'll also be documenting the process for yourself if you want to look back at how you got started.

Showcase Your Delicious Food

Your food is where your videos should create the most buzz! Make videos of every item on your menu. Your food videos should make the viewer hungry! I know I've watched many recipe videos that made my stomach growl. Yours should do the same. Make sure you get shots of people enjoying your dishes, and you and your staff cooking it.

But to really make people get hungry for your creations, you need to shoot close-ups of your food. Get shots of it plated or in a bowl. Add condiments to it or stir it around. If your food is wrapped in paper, make sure to unwrap it slowly in your video when you reveal what's inside. Wraps and sandwiches should be cut in half so the viewer can really see what's inside.

Introduce Your Staff Members

Your staff is important to you, and they are the ones that will be interacting with your customers. So it makes sense to shoot a few videos that feature your staff members. This way, your customers will see a familiar face when they come to your truck. This sense of familiarity will make your customers feel like they kind of know who they'll be ordering from.

You could include biographical information about your staff and have them tell some interesting facts about themselves. This can lead to a more conversational interaction between your employees and customers. Have them share their interests on the camera. Do they have a pet? Feature the pets in the video. Different aspects of the video will appeal to different people. You don't have to include everything in one video. And I think sometimes it's best to split some of this information into two or more videos so you'll have more content to post.

Have your employees tell their story of the work they do on your food truck. If you don't have employees, then use these ideas on yourself and co-owners. I know some of you operate with no hired staff. But you should still make yourself personable so customers will recognize you and want to meet you. In essence, you're starting to build your relationship with customers before they come to your truck.

Demonstrate How You Prepare Your Food

Another type of video you can make is a demonstration video. For food truck owners or anyone in the food and drink industry, you'd typically make cooking videos. So it makes sense to show and explain how you cook your food. This doesn't mean you have to give away the recipe but your customers might be interested in how your food is prepared. When customers see you preparing your recipes, you can create a better connection when they come to visit your truck. How much you actually reveal in your recipe videos depends on your comfort level.

You can even make videos of your shopping trips. For example, it would be easy to get some shots at a farmers market where you're selecting the ingredients for the day. You could show how to assemble a giant sandwich or how you garnish a dish. There are many possibilities!

Make Recap Videos

After you attend a special event, you can make a video that highlights the best part of being there. You may not have time to shoot video, but even if you have time to snap a few pictures, they can be used to string together a quick video slideshow. Another idea is to invite a friend to the event and shoot some video for you with a video camera or even just their smartphone. Tell them you'll feed them if they do this favor for you. Most people wouldn't turn down free food!

The video or pictures shown in this type of video should establish the location and atmosphere of the event. But don't forget to highlight your truck and the food you are serving. Showing viewers where you are is great but remember that this video still intended to promote your truck, your food and your business more than anything else.

You should also thank your hosts or at least say some grateful words about your location or venue in your video. When the video is done and uploaded to YouTube, don't forget to share a link to your clients so that they can share it via their social media sites like Facebook and Twitter.

Respond to Comments

Since YouTube is a social media platform, viewers can and will leave comments under your videos. This is another place where you can engage with your customers and build a better connection. When others see you replying to the comments, they'll immediately get the impression that you are accessible and approachable.

You don't have to have YouTube message alerts turned on (I don't), but I do log in once a week to check comments and respond to any comments that need replies. This is my way of batching the task of commenting on YouTube.

Customize Your Channel

Make your YouTube channel attractive to subscribers by uploading a cover image. This is the big banner that appears at the top of your channel page. The image size required is 2560x1440 pixels. However, the actual area of that image shown will vary depending on the device the viewer is using. This seems quite weird to me because it seems like a lot of the image is cut off most of the time. There is a logo/text safe zone right in the middle of the 2560x1440 image that is visible on all devices, but as I said before, any graphical information outside of the safe zone can and will be cut off on different devices.

The next important thing to do with your channel is to group similar videos together. YouTube allows you to create sections that can contain playlists with titles. For example, if you have multiple recipe videos, create a section called Recipes and start linking your recipe videos into that section or playlist. When you get several sections organized, the viewer will see a more polished looking channel and is more likely to subscribe to your channel.

People who click the subscribe button will be taken to the channel page first. So if your channel looks unorganized and random, you may have a more difficult time gaining subscribers. I have several channels but I still need to organize the one that has the most videos. There are about 60 videos I've uploaded to my channel, but when I go to my channel page, it only shows the last 4 videos. So to the viewer, it looks like I only have four videos when, in fact, I have quite a bit more. I think that's part of the reason why my own subscriber count is going up so slowly right now.

Marketing Lessons from Food Trucks

Food Trucks have been springing up all over the nation. Everything scrumptiously sinful is on a truck. From cake shakes and fried Oreos to ginger Brussels grows and Short Rib Sandwiches...

They Make a Standout Brand Personality

The truck proprietors put a great deal of thought into thinking of an innovative name and overall theme. The decals and truck configuration can make or break them. Some keep it basic and focus on making great food; others go insane with characters and graffiti-like structure. Just like in any business, standing out from your rivals is vital.

Most of Them Get the Word Out with Social Media

Food Truck proprietors use Facebook and Twitter since they move around a lot so that individuals can track them down. (Most of my friends find out about Food Trucks on Twitter or Facebook and read reviews on which ones are ideal.)

About 75 Percent of Food Trucks Have Qr Codes

While individuals remain in line they ordinarily have their smart phones in their grasp. Food Truck proprietors ask that they scan the QR code to tail them on Facebook and Twitter, so they get the most recent updates.

Missed Opportunity

Few trucks have 4" X 6" Flyers with QR Codes connected to Facebook, Twitter, their site, and telephone number. For what reason aren't the proprietors approaching individuals to sign up for an email list? Missed chance? Why not gather their data and send them updates once per week about up and coming occasions.

Reviews

Like most people, I have most loved Food Trucks. I'm fixated on this scrumptious, scrumdiddlyumptious (no genuine word can portray how great it is) Short Rib Sandwich. I talk about it on Facebook, and my companions have all attempted it! Many individuals post reviews on Yelp or their own sites, so it's a smart thought to urge clients to review your business. A few trucks have a decal requesting that clients review them on Yelp.

CHAPTER 13. TIPS TO KEEP THE FOOD TRUCK RUNNING

The launchpad is ready to release, and it is time to rev up the engines and stoves of the food truck. Marketing is absolutely essential to keep any business running. You should help the business to get noticed so that you can lure in customers. Competitors in the same field of business are never going to rest and make it easier for you. It is important that you advertise and market yourself and your food product efficiently. Here are some marketing tips for the food truck business:

Set up Weekly Specials

After the launch, it is important that you gain speed and traffic in business. If a customer likes a specific food item like a Mexican taco, you could have "Taco Tuesdays" where you serve the customers tacos at half the normal price. This will spread the word and will assure you a lot of people.

Be One with the Community

Get close to the community you want to serve. Sponsor for a local sports event or try helping in a charity. Also, find ways to tie up with other business owners in the community.

Hold Contests

People love contests, and they are an excellent idea to promote your food truck business. Promote the contests through social media and other forms of advertising.

Celebrate Often

You do not need a big reason to celebrate. Opt for smaller holidays and make things exciting and new for the customers. Show the spirit of your celebration through the food you offer.

Have an Inner Circle

Treat your most valuable customers nicely and create an inner circle with them. Offer them discounts and earn their trust by being sweet and nice to them.

After all this, it is also important that you choose the perfect spot to put up the food truck. Make sure that you choose a place where there will be a lot of hungry people. Park your vehicle next to a commercial or industrial space. Also, make sure that there are no serious competitors around to spoil your day. When you want to choose a place, also find out about the events that might happen regularly at that place. Try to participate in such events and maximize your profit in doing so. Assure that you find out about the ease in which you can get the licenses to put up your food truck in these events. Do not feel bad about partnering up. Partner up with a mall or building complex that will allow you to set up a spot on their property.

Feel Free to Market Yourself

Marketing extends beyond the beginning phase, and it is essential to keep the food truck running. Take advantage of digital media and its marketing platforms. Tweet about the places you are going to put up the stall, connect with Facebook, and maintain a Facebook page to post regular updates. Have a well-planned social media marketing scheme and try to lure in more customers by showing the merrier sides in dining with you. Also, make sure that you deliver the quality and service that you have advertised. False advertising can put a hole in the whole process easier.

Think Freely and Do Not Attach Yourself to an Idea

Even if you have found the perfect spot for business and even it had worked well for a long time, there is a possibility of dwindling of sales. Take time to re-plan and think about moving to another new area. Do not be too rigid in the way you think. It is a waste of time, and you might end up losing the business in the process.

Expand on the Revenue Stream

Change over the course of time and try implementing new business ideas. Take risks and always be on the lookout for new opportunities. Cater to events and festivals to increase the profits you take. Get out of the comfort zone and try new and exciting things. Keep the energy and the flow running.

Be Open to Teaming Up

Do not feel bad about teaming up with other food truck owners out there. You could really get a lot out of it, because people who eat out of food trucks are most likely to change their trucks often. Pick a crowded place and a friendly food truck owner to club your business with. Cater to that crowded place together and get the best out of that situation. It need not be on a regular basis, but it is good to team up once in a while. People will also love the variety that you and your friend in business have to offer.

Keep Networking

Make friends with people who have a strong influence over the place. Drop the prejudice and consider asking other truck owners to get valuable referrals for events and festivals. People might help you, and you might even expand your network. Do not live in your own world and miss out on the exposure that others have to offer to you.

Make a Good Investment in Your Staff

Make sure that you help the staff grow within their positions so that they stay trustworthy and faithful in the future. It is important that you treat them with the respect that they deserve, and it is vital that you acknowledge their good work. The process of bringing in and training new staff is not only time-consuming but also costly.

Put a Good Price Tag on Your Food Items

Even if you are new to the business, it is not necessary that you have to offer food for a very cheap rate. If your food is tasty and has very good quality, feel free to charge the price that will benefit your system. It is vital to remember that people are ready to pay for the good stuff. Keep your eyes on the quality of the food you serve, and you will see a growth in business automatically.

These tips and techniques are essential in your path to become a successful food truck owner. So, get out there and put out some interesting items on the menu to keep the hungry taste buds on fire. Serve with a bright smile on your face and complete love in your heart. There are a whole lot of people to feed in this world, and it is high time that you realize that you can be the change you want to see. Thrive and work hard to serve the tastiest food on wheels and make sure that you touch the lives of people with what you do.

Instagram

Instagram is based on images, so depending on your business, this could be a great way to get your name out there. Hashtags are also big on Instagram, so be sure to include your business hashtag on everything! #BusinessShark

You can also pay to advertise on Instagram, although it costs nothing to join.

Twitter

Twitter is based on short messages up to 280 characters long. This is great for promoting events and coupons! You should also use hashtags here on this free platform. Pay to advertise here as well.

LinkedIn

LinkedIn is social media for professionals. It is good to have a presence here as well, especially if you are marketing to businesses. There are LinkedIn groups you can get into that may help you as you begin your entrepreneurship journey. Paid advertisements are an option, and joining is free like the others.

CHAPTER 14. PROFITS AND EXPENSES

W hile a food truck has the advantage of moving to where the customers are, they also have the disadvantage of breaking down. Even the slightest problems require a reliable mechanic to fix problems before they arise.

There are almost an unlimited number of mechanics available for most vehicle repairs, but generally less for food truck repairs, depending on the problem and location. That's why it is important to be proactive and find a few reliable truck mechanics ahead of time before you actually run into problems.

When looking for reliable truck repair, consider speaking with friends or even competitors that you can trust. Search for references of those who use certain mechanics regularly to find someone who is honest and reliable. Also, check online feedback when possible.

With kitchen issues, it may be best to once again speak with competitors you can trust or suppliers who may know someone that can help repair the specific equipment you're having issues with.

The purpose of your business is likely to make a living doing what you love. So many people have a strong creative side, but not always a strong business sense. That is not impossible to change! The purpose of Business Shark books is to teach entrepreneurs how to succeed in business and in life.

You will find countless books on sales, on how to get out of debt, how to become rich, and work a few hours a week. They are all valuable! Some of the best advice out there is to ensure you are making a profit and invest that profit. You want to be sure that you can take care of yourself and your family no matter what happens with this business. Building profit into everything you do will ensure that!

As discussed before, you want to build profit into your prices. You also need to build your salary into pricing. Profit is on top of your salary! There is no set percentage but try to start at ten percent. If there is room for more, go for it.

When you are closing your books for the day, determine how much profit there was. Keep a running tab, and at least twice a month, make a deposit into your high-interest savings account. This is now your investment account. It is recommended to keep that money there until you reach the two-year mark or until you have three months expenses saved. You must plan for emergencies, and if your business floods or you have a fire or any unexpected event that causes you to close, you need to have that money available.

Once you have money saved over the three month's expenses, or you have passed the two-year mark (when you can get good financing), you should invest your money. How you invest, it is up to you. Many experts say real estate is the safest and most profitable investment around. Others like a little more risk and play the stock market. Perhaps you want to open a second location or expand your current location.

When you get to the point of investing, you can start to relax a little as you are building your wealth now. Hopefully, by now, you have paid down some debts and are comfortable in your successful business. You are on the path to financial independence!

Making a Profit

Whether a food truck is born from the mind of an aspiring chef or from an entrepreneur, making a profit is the key to success and often why they get into this industry.

But if you think that the profits are just going to come rolling in as soon as you open, you'd better think again! Owning and maintaining a successful food truck generally requires long hours, lots of competition, and a lot of legal issues that vary from state-to-state. You may have seen popular food trucks in your city or watched television programs that portray the glamorous side of the mobile food industry. Seeing these examples might make you think how hard can this be? What you don't see is the work each of those owners had to go through to get to where they're at now.

Starting a food truck is like starting any kind of business. You have to build it up from nothing. And the first couple of years are probably going to be the hardest you've ever worked just to scrape up an income to pay for your initial expenses.

This is not to scare you away from starting your own food truck business because there are definitely profits to be made. According to Off the Grid's Matthew Cogen, most trucks make $250,000 to $500,000 each year. And industry experts already calculate major growth in this multi-billion dollar industry.

Surviving the Winter Months

For most gourmet food trucks, there is one obstacle food truck owners must face every year... unless you happen to live in a warm-weather region. Food truck owners will often tell you that they find themselves struggling during winter months. Unlike a brick-and-mortar business, the number of customers you have during the winter months will dwindle down to almost nothing. When your food truck business seems to be slowing down to conditions where it doesn't make sense to even open, there are several alternative venues to consider in order to keep your business afloat during the cold months.

One option would be catering. Instead of searching for customers in the cold, you should look for clients or events that will bring customers to you. Start advertising as a catering business during summer months and then reach out to cater parties and events year-round.

In addition to parties and events, try partnering with offices and other businesses to serve their needs. Look for tournaments and conventions that need catering. For some food truck owners, winter months may even be more profitable than summer months.

For those who are still willing to work outside, consider mixing up the menu during the winter months. Bring in coffees and hot chocolates to the menu to boost sales, keeping your customers warm during the off-season.

You should embrace the mobility of a food truck. There is no reason to stay in one location. Move to businesses that need catering or extra choices during winter months and look for big events near you that could use additional choices in terms of unique and quality meals.

In the end, it is your decision whether or not to stay open during winter. Plenty of other businesses make their money in summer months and take winters off. But if you do close down for the winter, you need to keep focusing on how you can improve business and profits the following season.

Unexpected Expenses

Just like the basic expenses of a restaurant, food trucks have other expenses to consider. With gas prices consistently increasing, your fuel costs can add up to be a hefty expense.

When parking your truck for business, finding a profitable spot can also often result in receiving a parking fine if you're not careful. Parking in the wrong location can result in massive expenses, with parking tickets each costing up to $130 or more. Some food truck owners consider this the "cost of doing business," but generally, it is not a good practice.

Weather conditions can also cause problems for food trucks. If customers are hoping to stay out of the rain, they may also avoid your truck, despite passing by your truck on their daily routine.

In addition, storage space can increase more and more throughout the year. Even vendors who cook on-site will need to prepare certain ingredients in a commissary or commercial kitchen, which often requires additional storage facilities.

CHAPTER 15. QUALITIES THAT A FOOD TRUCK VENDOR MUST HAVE

In the past, individuals thought of food trucks as a source of junk food. Anyway, as time passed by, the value and the functionality of food trucks have been uncovered. Individuals who are swamped at work and have no opportunity to take their lunch in the solaces of their homes or eateries rely on food truck proprietors to bring them healthy meals.

In view of the notoriety of vending trucks, few people who might need to earn are venturing to this kind of business. If you wish to be a successful food truck trader, you should have the following attitudes:

Patient

Finding a vehicle that you can transform into a vending truck involves a great deal of time. There are a lot of organizations that sell vehicles that are perfect for being converted into food trucks. If you lack the patience in scouring the market for the best deal that you can get, at that point, you might be deceived by merchants who take advantage of the high demand for vehicles. If you need to set aside cash and get the best vehicle, you should be able to look for the best deal.

Hard-Working

A food seller should be productive. Being innovative means being to get the same number of requests as you can from the workplaces that are situated at places where your food truck will pass on. If the seller is innovative, then he will be able to convey his products to numerous workplaces and offices.

Friendly

It is significant that you can assemble affinity with your clients. This is because if they consider you to be a well-known face and a businessperson who considers nothing but profits. Friendliness means you selling a greater amount of your merchandise and items.

Creative

Clients don't care for routine food. This is the reason why they would avoid heading off to the office cafeteria to eat their meals. You should be creative in your menus. Ensure that you have an assortment of food that you can offer to your clients. It won't just satisfy your clients, however, you will likewise be able to remain in front of your competition.

Manage Time Successfully

You should recall that the basic reason why you are starting a food truck business is for the adaptability and freedom rather than simply being positioned in one location. If you can manage your time well, then you can serve numerous clients. The more places you can visit in one day, the more clients, the more profits you gain.

The food truck business is anything but a difficult business to learn. If you have every one of these attributes, then you will unquestionably become wildly successful.

CHAPTER 16. PITFALLS TO AVOID

M any people are jumping into the food truck industry, expecting to build a business that they can grow and profit from. It is undoubtedly a very exciting and high-profile type of business. New food truck owners are hitting the streets for the first time every month across the country. While the industry is still growing, it is an unfortunate reality that not every food truck owner is going to make a sustainable living at this. There aren't reliable statistics as to how many food truck businesses fail each year, but some experts estimate that the failure rate is upwards of around 60% during the first three years of business. This is about the same rate at which restaurants fail.

Before you start doubting the merits of the food truck industry, you should be aware of some of the factors surrounding those failures. That way, the warning signs can be recognized earlier, and preventative action can be taken. There are a lot of misconceptions or lack of knowledge for those who enter this industry. Many believe that just because they are a good cook means they can successfully run a food truck. While being able to create delicious tasting dishes is an integral part of a successful food truck, owners must realize that it is still a business that needs to be treated as a business. It's not necessarily a business you can invest in and just hire people to run it... at least not in the beginning. It takes a lot of hours and hard work to build up a customer base. A lot of growing pains are realized in the early years. And above all, costs need to be effectively managed.

Outsiders do not realize the amount of unseen work that goes into the daily operation of a food truck. There are many hours of preparation time like sourcing ingredients, location scouting, marketing, cooking, packaging, and more. In most cases, food truck owners are involved in every aspect of the daily routine and must be prepared and understand this fact. The time commitment alone is enough for some food truck owners to shut down in the first year. Anything worth building takes time to nurture and refine.

A great practice we can borrow from small to medium size restaurants is to keep your menu at a manageable size. Your truck has limited storage space as well as kitchen space. Too many items on your menu mean you need more space to store your raw ingredients. If your truck is theme-based, then only offer the most popular dishes for the style of food you are serving. That way, you can excel at a few dishes and maintain consistency. If you are cooking too many unique items, orders can get mixed up and cause confusion in the kitchen.

Making customers wait can lead to negative feelings toward your truck. Avoid offering dishes that take too long to prepare. Customers who visit food trucks generally expect relatively fast service, especially if they've been standing in a long line. In addition, the more people you can move through your line, the greater the profits. Having an efficient process from taking the customer's order to delivering the plated dish greatly benefits you and the customer.

Unexpected expenses can also kill an otherwise promising food truck operation. The daily costs of staying open can make it appear that money is flying out the door constantly. But when you have to pay for unplanned expenses, things really start to get tight. You're already paying for a commissary, propane, ingredients, serving supplies, staffing, and more! But often, vehicle maintenance gets overlooked. It is inevitable that your food truck will break down. Whether it is the truck itself or the equipment, any kind of repair is costly. To keep costs down, most food truck owners buy old trucks that are prone to mechanical failure. Some vehicle expenses can be manageable, but big break downs like transmission failure can severely put a dent in your revenue.

A lack of understanding of new technology can also contribute to the demise of a food truck owner. A mobile food entrepreneur needs to have a firm grasp of how social media like Twitter and Facebook can benefit a business. Social media platforms need to work in tandem with your traditional marketing efforts. Maintaining consistency in your cooking, locations, and customer service leads to happy customers that know what to expect each time they visit you.

Building and growing a reliable customer base takes time and constant nurturing. Having poor customer service can also turn new and existing customers away. A single case of poor treatment of a customer can lead to very damaging criticism on sites like Yelp and Urbanspoon. Customers who have never even tried your truck may brush you off without even sampling your food.

Like anything in life, you only get one chance to make a first impression, so make sure you have the right person interacting with your customers. Understanding where the points of failure can come from will better prepare you for these types of situations. Building a successful food truck is not a get rich quick type of business. Hard work, a sound business plan, and proper financial management are the solid foundation for any food truck entrepreneur. While it cannot guarantee success, it will give you an advantage over those that are not as well prepared!

CONCLUSION

F ood truck marketing isn't an exact science, but it does require creativity, ingenuity, patience and persistence. When done right it can be a huge asset for your business. Marketing your food truck helps your business relate to the community and your customers. It helps build your brand and your reputation.

A great marketing plan positions your business as an authority in your field. But it isn't a one-time task. Marketing your food truck is an ongoing process that starts long before you launch your truck and goes through the life of the business. It's geared to gain you new customers while keeping the ones you've already captured with your fantastic food.

If you don't have a marketing plan, start now using the techniques outlined in this book. Ideally, you've been marketing since the start of your business, but you need to start now so you can grow your business even larger. It's a process that can evolve over time, but it should be at the forefront of your outreach to customers. Try new things and definitely stretch your creativity. Definitely employ the feedback from others, and get marketing advice from professionals if you don't know where to turn.

You want your food truck to survive for the long haul, so exercising patience is a trait an entrepreneur needs to have. You will face many challenges. You will have fun times. And you will be frustrated. But a true entrepreneur can overcome all the challenges. You're ready for that, right?

Enthusiasm is probably the most important single-word line of advice that can be given on the topic of how to be a successful food truck operator. Whether your passion is for the food or for the money, so long as you have passion, you'll have success.

Don't limit yourself to just parking and setting up shop. Stay connected with the community and abreast of upcoming events like concerts and festivals. Even though you may pay a fee to use these grounds, the payoff could be tremendous. If you've built a great reputation for your food truck, then event organizers may even pay you for your presence at their events.

Food truck marketing combines traditional techniques with the latest high-tech methods to communicate with your community. This is an exciting time to be in the food truck industry. If you're a technical person, then you will have a blast using social media, but even if you're not, you'll still have fun and will be able to learn the tools available to you easily. Pay attention to what your competition is doing and start out by emulating their methods. Over time, you will be able to modify those techniques and mold them to fit your own food truck business.

This is your dream! This is your business! Take charge of your marketing efforts, and the results will speak for themselves! Reach out and connect with your customers so they will remember you and your food. Good luck, and I wish you all the success you deserve!

Join associations and organizations like the chamber of commerce and keep networking. Once you've achieved a certain level of success, you should spend most of your time outside of the truck developing new business opportunities and growing your brand. Meanwhile, make sure you have some reliable and competent employees who can hold down the fort when you're away.